T0190730

Adrienne Barman

CREATUREPEDIA

WELCOME TO THE GREATEST SHOW ON EARTH

WIDE EYED EDITIONS

Contents

CREATUREPEDIA celebrates the amazing array of animals that grace our planet. Sadly, some are now under threat, some are already extinct (and one or two may never have existed in the first place!), but each one has its own unique part to play in the animal kingdom...

Turn the page to see the greatest show on Earth and discover who is the biggest, the brainiest, and the most beautiful of them all.

The architects

Social weaver
builds the largest nest of any bird

The architects

Beaver
builds a dam from logs, mud, and stones to keep predators away

Weaver ant
works with others to weave leaves together to make a nest

Prairie dog burrow has sleeping chambers, nursery chambers, and chambers for hiding from hunters

Taveta weaver male weaver builds nest, female chooses mate based on quality of nest

Spider spins a strong web

Mason wasp female builds a tiny mud nest, stocked with food for each of her eggs

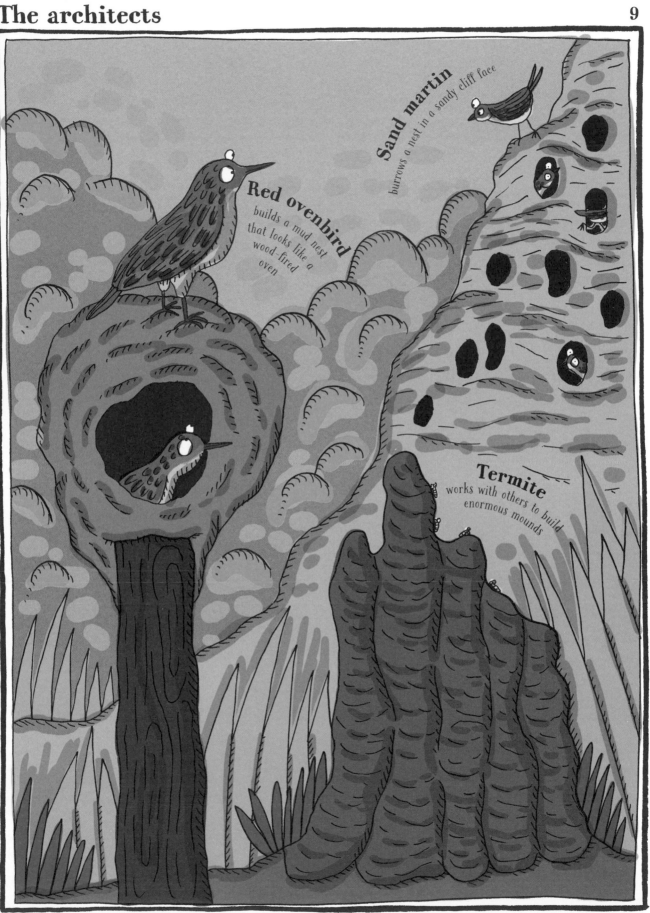

Sand martin
burrows a nest in a sandy cliff face

Red ovenbird
builds a mud nest that looks like a wood-fired oven

Termite
works with others to build enormous mounds

The big-eared beasts

Black-tailed jackrabbit
ears detect predators and help jackrabbit keep cool

Fennec fox large ears give
off heat so fox stays cool in the desert

Gray long-eared bat
ears nearly the length of its body

Long-eared hedgehog
lives in hot deserts, so long ears help it keep cool by giving off heat

Aye-aye
finds food by tapping on trees, then using large ears to listen for grubs moving under the bark

Caracal
twitches long ear tufts to communicate with other caracals

Silvery marmoset
sometimes called the bare-ear marmoset

Koala
excellent hearing

Aardvark
large ears detect insects in the ground

Coyote
very powerful hearing to help it hunt

Serval uses long ears to listen for birds among tall grasses

Long-eared owl "ears" on top of head are actually just tufts of feathers; real ears are small openings close to eyes

Bushpig position of ears reveals mood: horizontal ears show aggression

The big mouths

Northern gannet

Helmeted guinea fowl

Natterjack toad

male call can be heard several miles away

Field cricket
makes sounds by rubbing its wings together

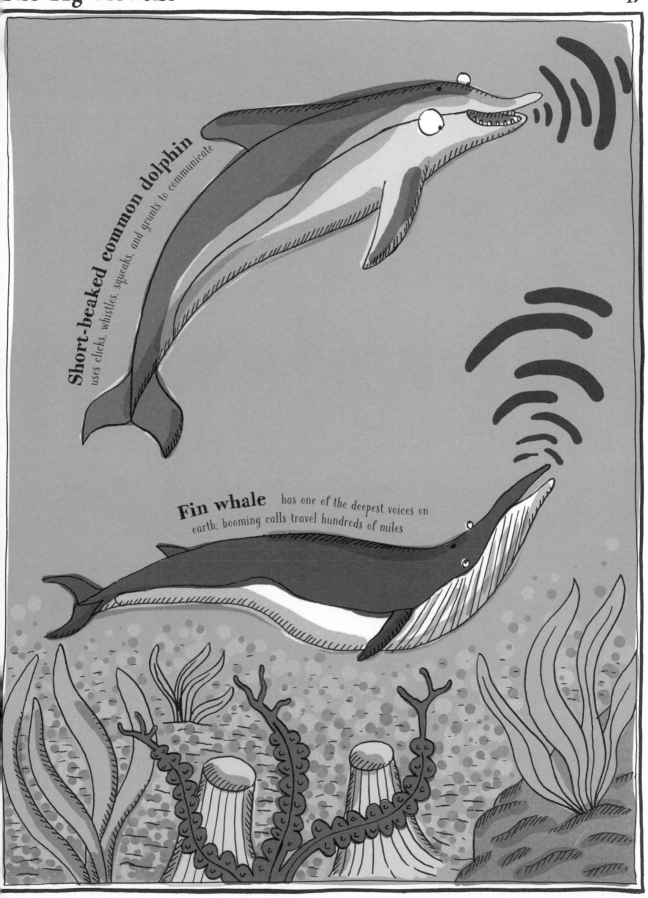

Short-beaked common dolphin uses clicks, whistles, squeaks, and grunts to communicate

Fin whale has one of the deepest voices on earth; booming calls travel hundreds of miles

Cicada
one of the noisiest insects in the world; can make a sound over 100 decibels!

Rattlesnake
has hollow segments on the end of its tail that knock together to make rattling sound

White-fronted goose

The blue beauties

Victoria crowned pigeon

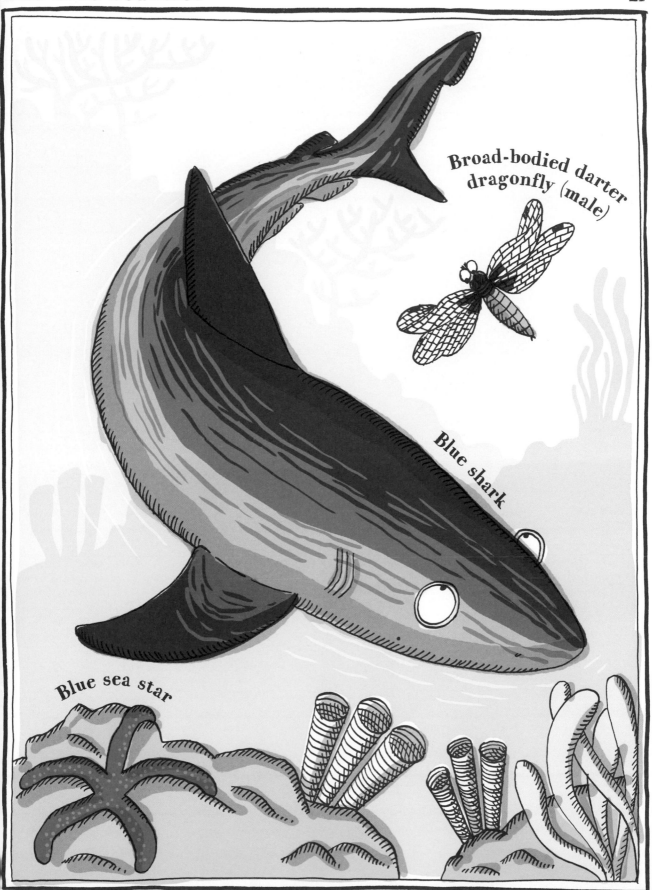

Broad-bodied darter dragonfly (male)

Blue shark

Blue sea star

The blue beauties

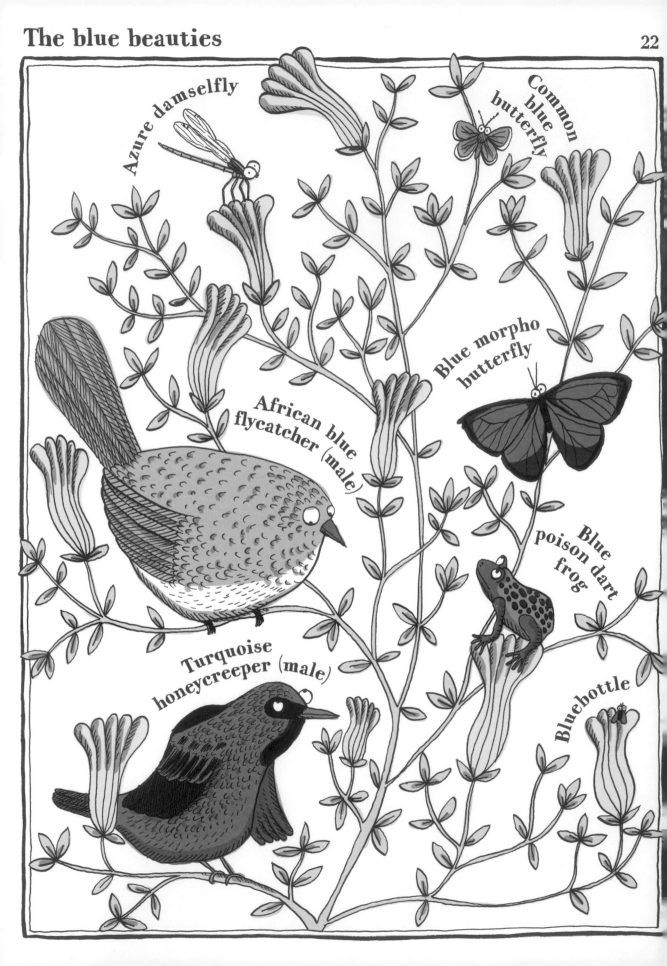

Azure damselfly

Common blue butterfly

Blue morpho butterfly

African blue flycatcher (male)

Blue poison dart frog

Turquoise honeycreeper (male)

Bluebottle

Rainbow agama (male)

Woodland kingfisher

Blue surgeonfish

Blue tit

Puma
can leap up to 20 feet
from a standing start

Kangaroo
the only large animal that uses jumping
as main means of getting around

Flying frog
glides between trees using large
webbed feet as parachutes

Atlantic salmon
leaps upstream to get to
breeding grounds

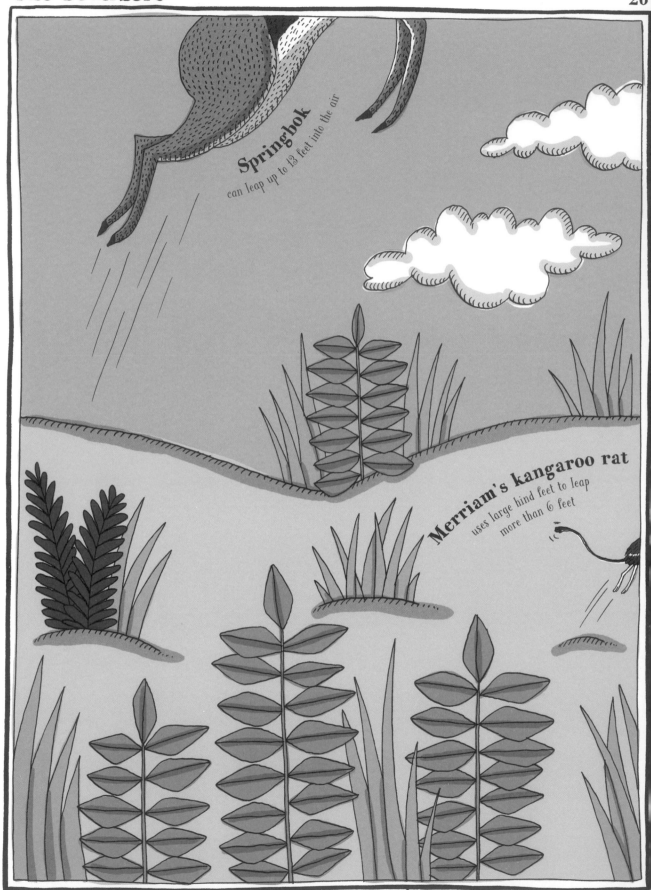

Springbok
can leap up to 13 feet into the air

Merriam's kangaroo rat
uses large hind feet to leap
more than 6 feet

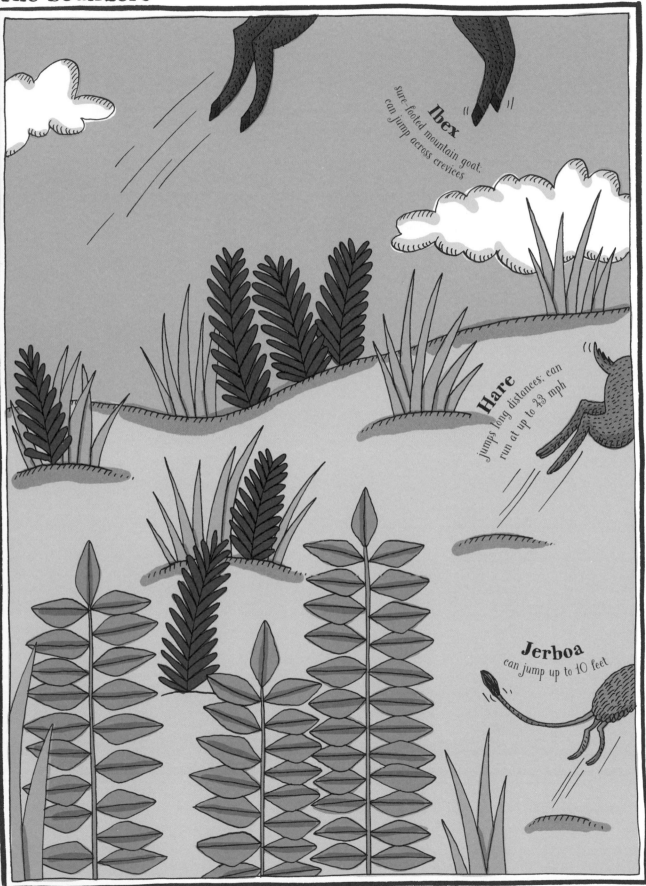

Ibex
sure-footed mountain goat;
can jump across crevices

Hare
jumps long distances; can
run at up to 43 mph

Jerboa
can jump up to 10 feet

The canary-yellows

Blue-cheeked butterfly fish

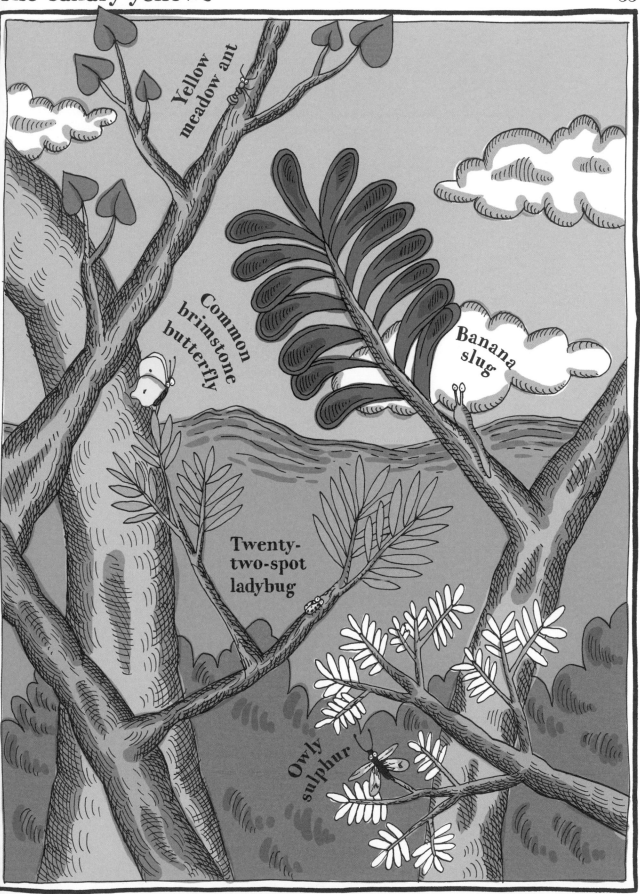

Yellow meadow ant

Common brimstone butterfly

Banana slug

Twenty-two-spot ladybug

Owly sulphur

The champion breath-holders

Walrus 30 minutes

The champion breath-holders

Elephant seal 100 minutes

Seal 100 minutes

Narwhal 30 minutes

Sperm whale 90 minutes

Hippopotamus
5 minutes

The coal-blacks

Carrion crow

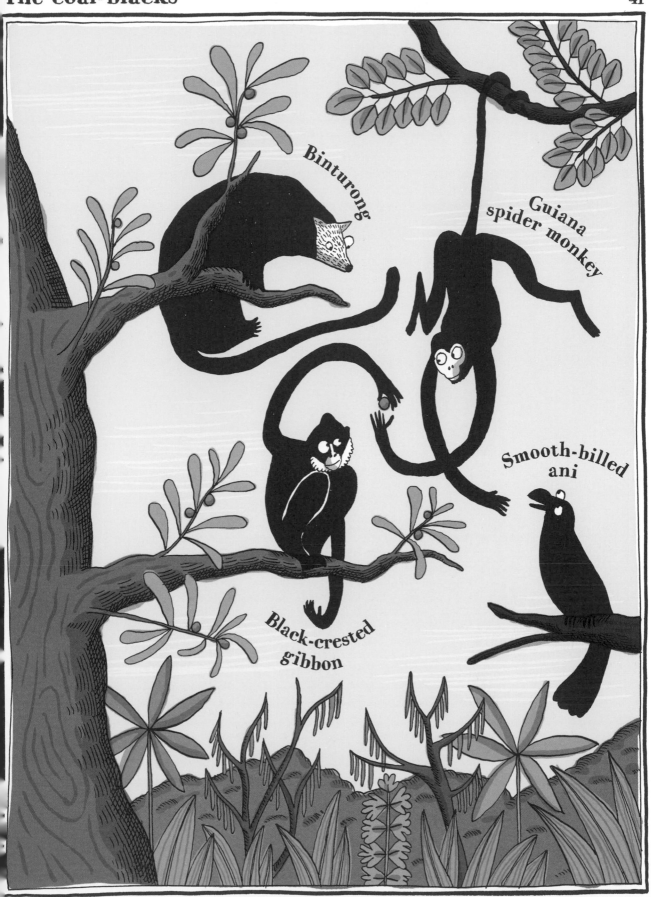

Binturong

Guiana
spider monkey

Smooth-billed
ani

Black-crested
gibbon

Black bear

Capricorn beetle

Violet ground beetle

Black panther

Black ant

Dung beetle

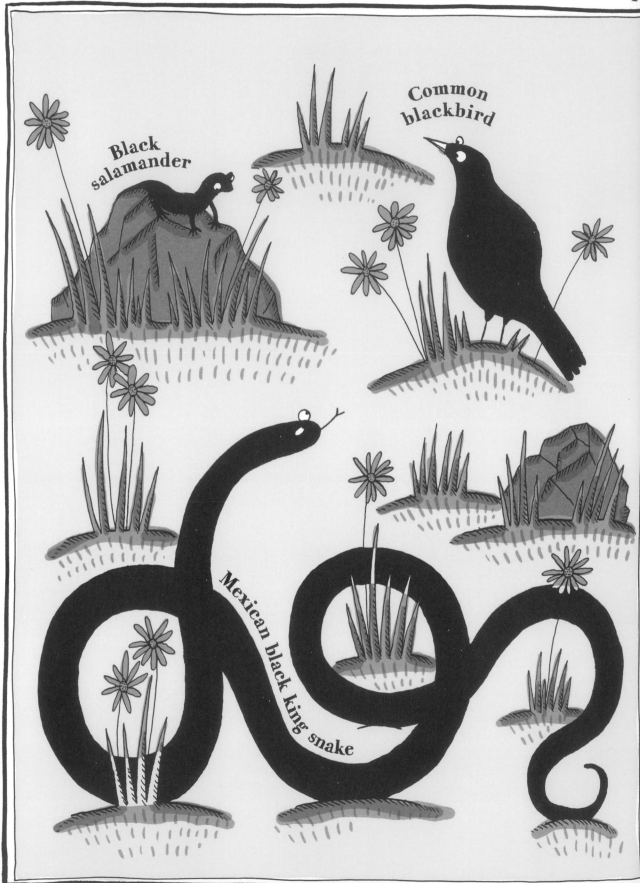

Black salamander

Common blackbird

Mexican black king snake

The endangered

Giant panda

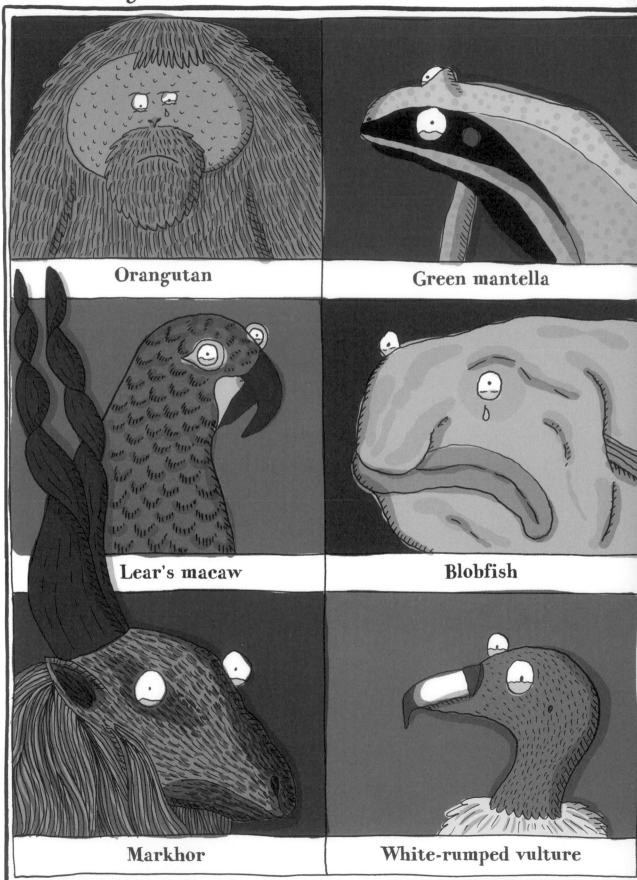

Orangutan

Green mantella

Lear's macaw

Blobfish

Markhor

White-rumped vulture

Southern cassowary

Saw-tailed bush cricket

Hawaiian monk seal

Drill

Basking shark

Chuckwalla

Chinese alligator

Corsican swallowtail

Asian arowana

Bobcat

Emerald damselfly

Ethiopian wolf

Snow leopard

Golden lion tamarin

Monkey-eating eagle

Hermit beetle

Green sea turtle

Otter

European green lizard

Kakapo

Rose chafer beetle

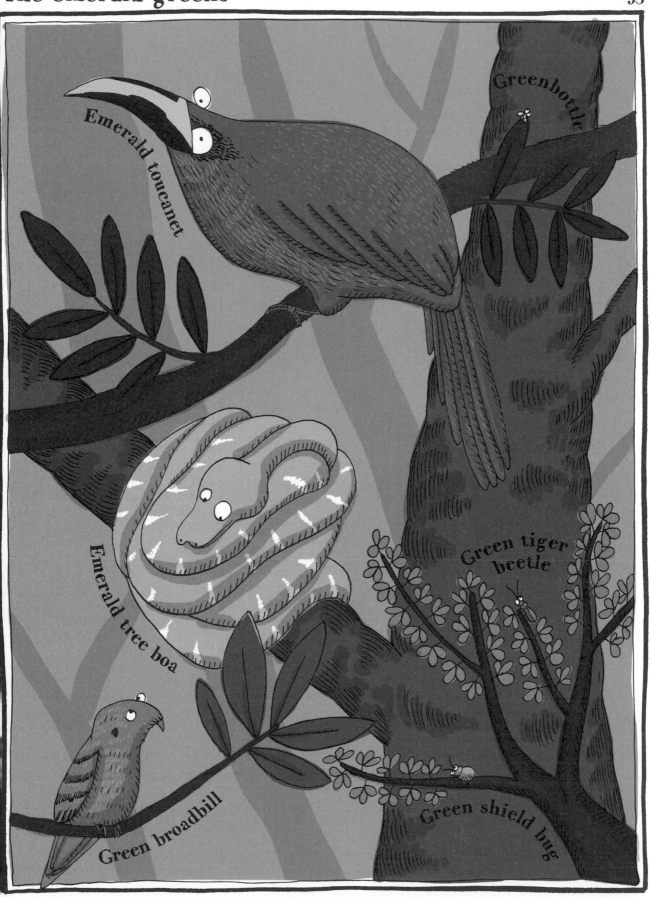

Emerald toucanet

Greenbottle

Emerald tree boa

Green tiger beetle

Green broadbill

Green shield bug

The faithful

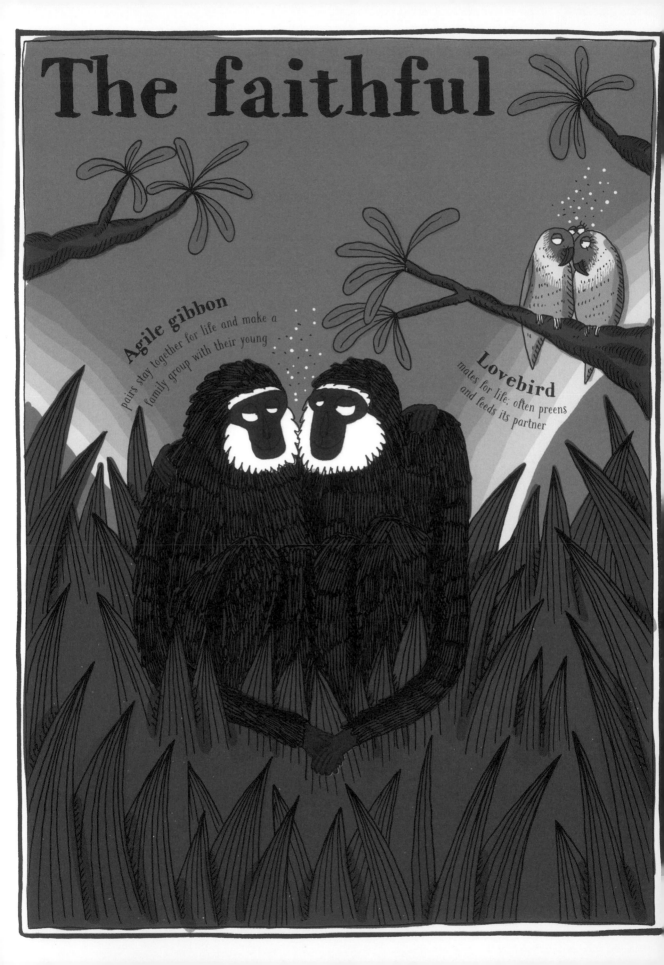

Agile gibbon
Pairs stay together for life and make a family group with their young

Lovebird
mates for life; often preens and feeds its partner

Dik-dik
pairs mate for life,
and are rarely seen apart

Wandering
albatross

Mongolian
gerbil

Whooper swan

Sea horse

Mandarin duck

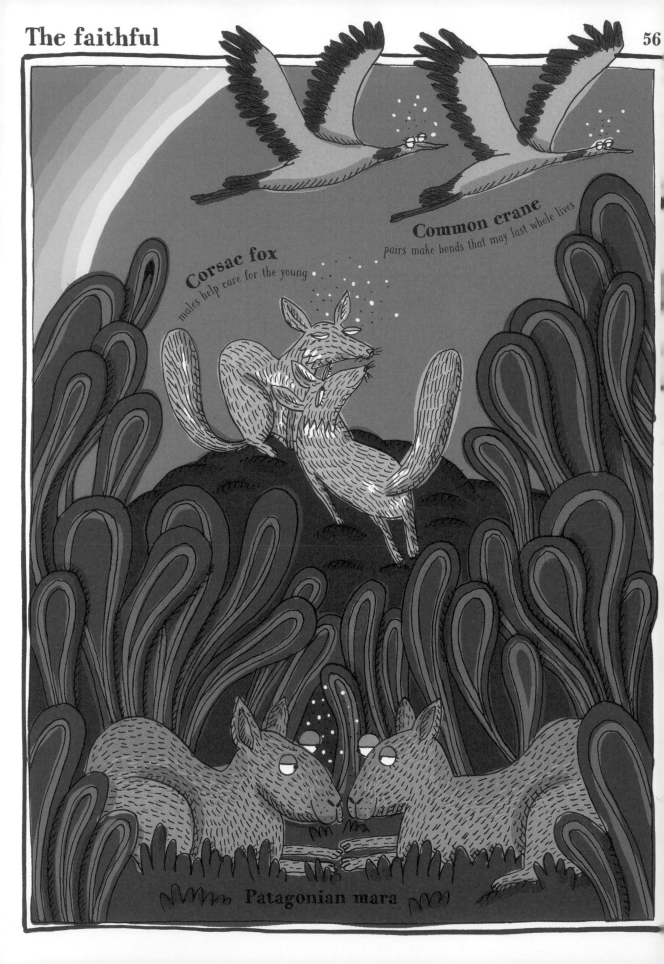

Common crane
pairs make bonds that may last whole lives

Corsac fox
males help care for the young

Patagonian mara

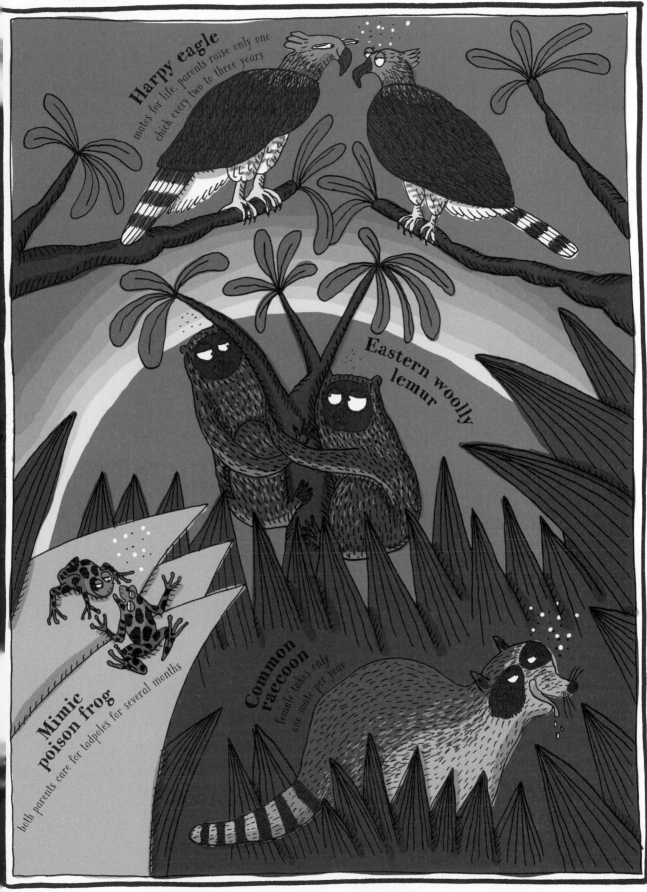

Harpy eagle
mates for life, parents raise only one
chick every two to three years

Eastern woolly lemur

Mimic poison frog
both parents care for tadpoles for several months

Common raccoon
female takes only
one mate per year

Our family friends

Sheep

Cormorant
used for fishing
in China

Donkey

European
rabbit

Chinchilla

Green iguana

Guinea
pig

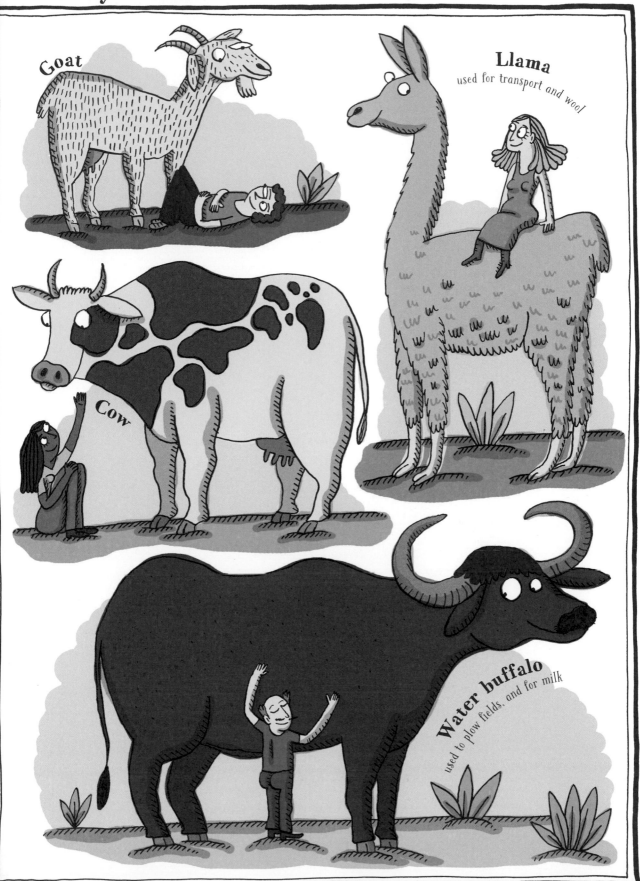

Goat

Llama
used for transport and wool

Cow

Water buffalo
used to plow fields, and for milk

Horse

Camel

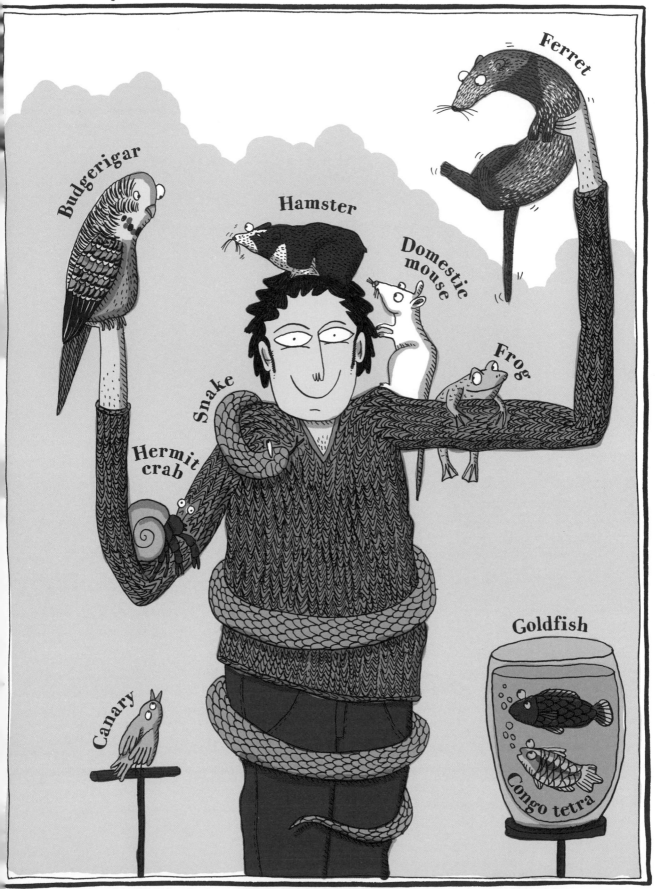

Ferret

Budgerigar

Hamster

Domestic mouse

Frog

Snake

Hermit crab

Goldfish

Canary

Congo tetra

The fierce

Sparrow hawk

Horsefly

Leech

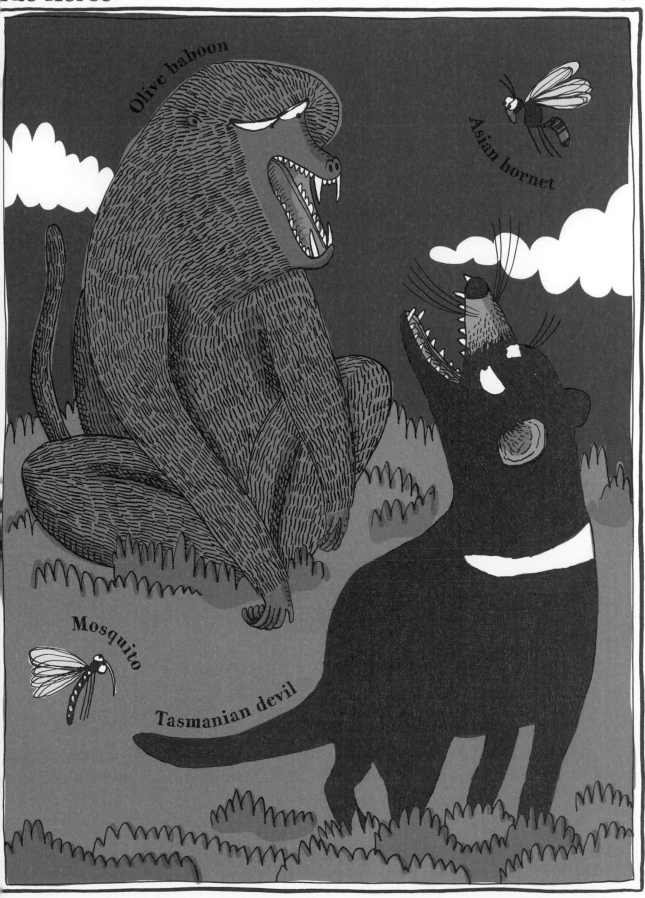

Olive baboon

Asian hornet

Mosquito

Tasmanian devil

Goliath tiger fish

Wels catfish

The fierce

Grizzly bear

Tick

Stoat

Kestrel

Inland taipan

The foresters

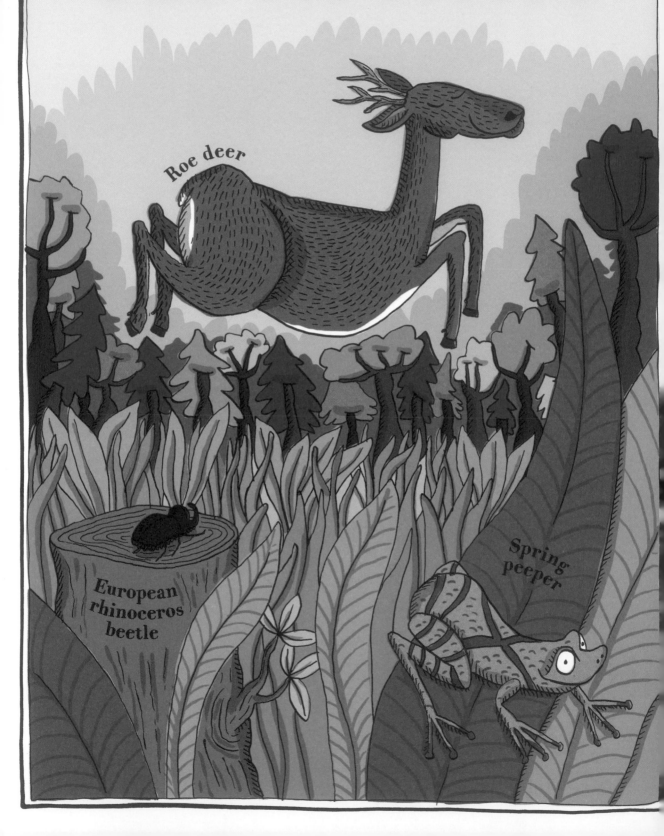

Roe deer

European rhinoceros beetle

Spring peeper

Indri

Loris

Grove
snail

Red squirrel

Emerald tree monitor

Edible dormouse

Valerio's glass frog

Sable

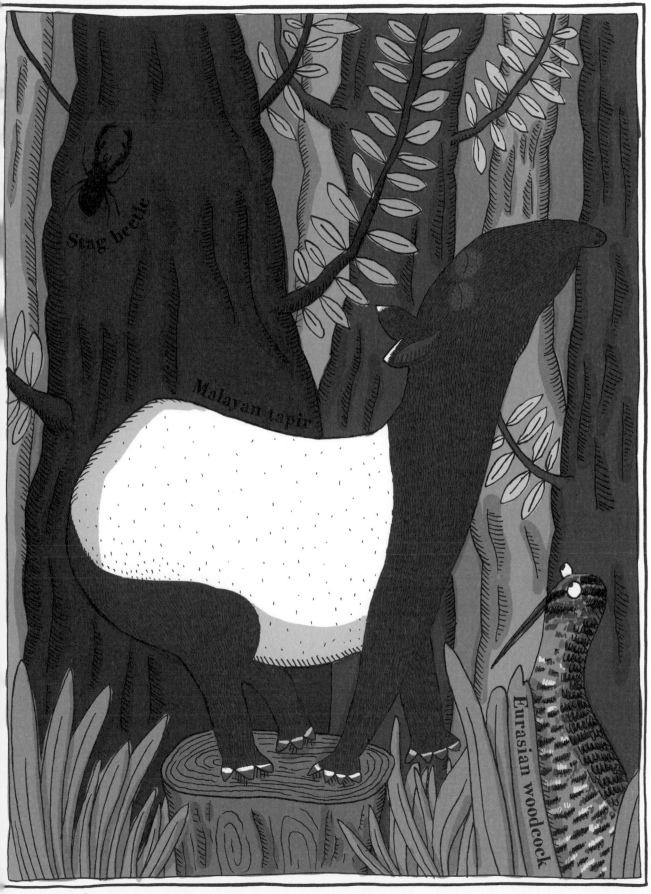

Stag beetle

Malayan tapir

Eurasian woodcock

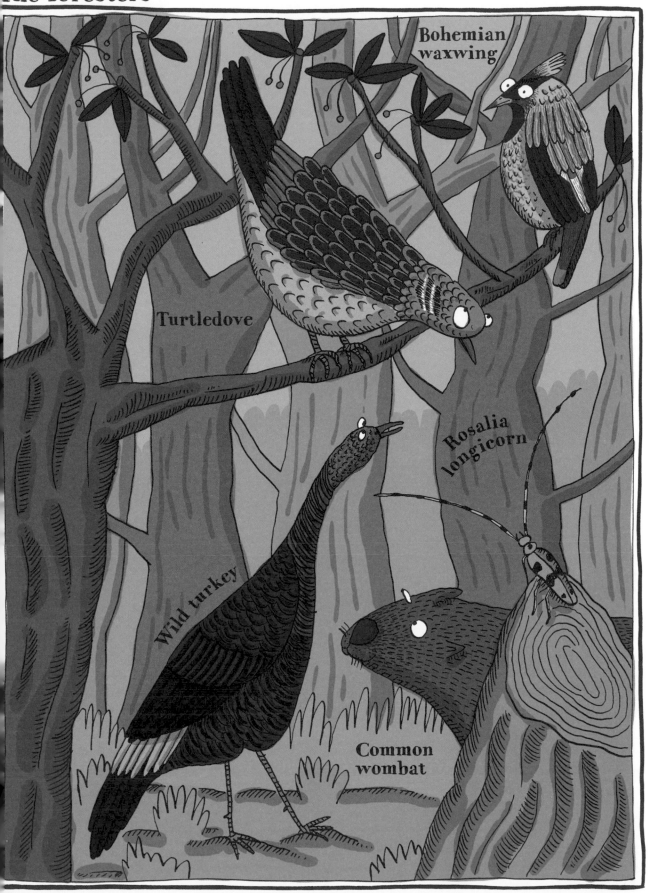

Bohemian waxwing

Turtledove

Rosalia longicorn

Wild turkey

Common wombat

The giants

Giant Pacific octopus

world's largest octopus: up to 30 feet across

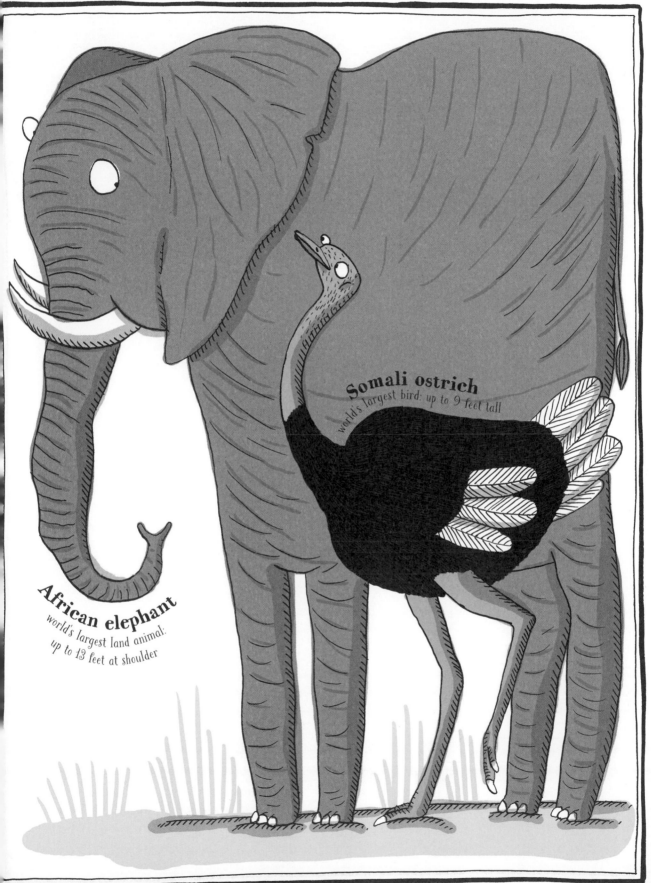

Somali ostrich
world's largest bird: up to 9 feet tall

African elephant
*world's largest land animal:
up to 13 feet at shoulder*

The giants

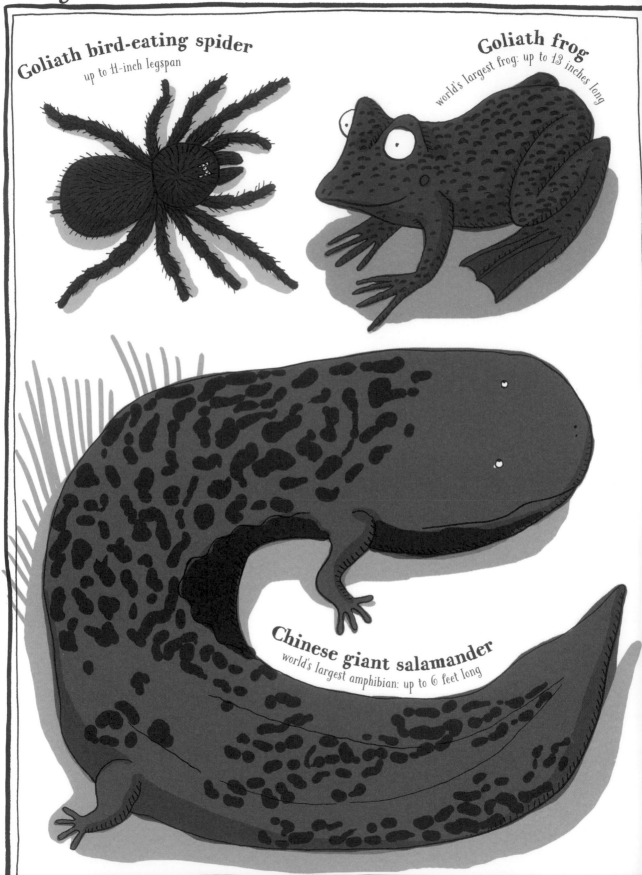

Goliath bird-eating spider
up to 11-inch legspan

Goliath frog
world's largest frog: up to 13 inches long

Chinese giant salamander
world's largest amphibian: up to 6 feet long

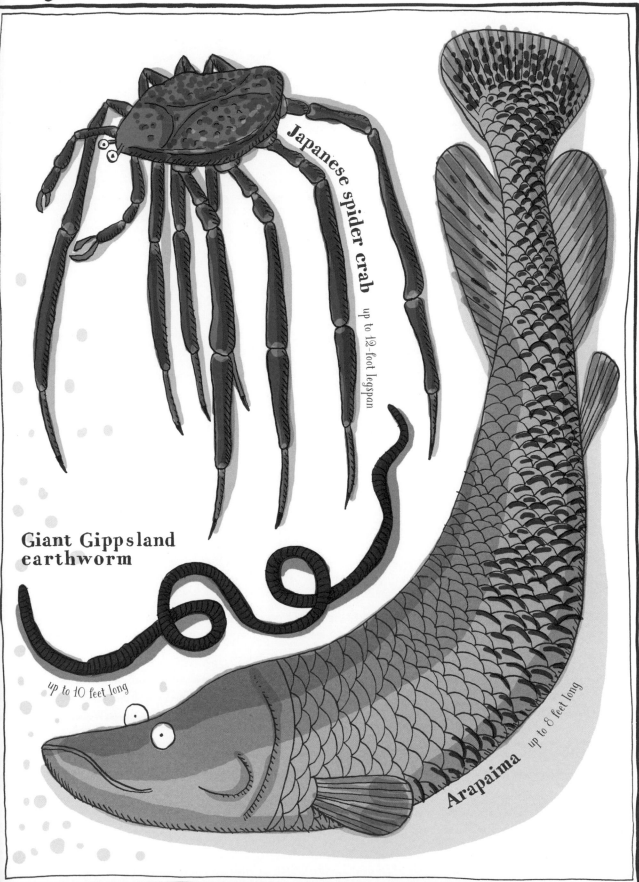

Japanese spider crab up to 12-foot legspan

Giant Gippsland earthworm

up to 10 feet long

Arapaima up to 8 feet long

The giants

Blue whale
largest animal ever to have lived: up to 108 feet long

Whale shark
world's largest fish: up to 40 feet long

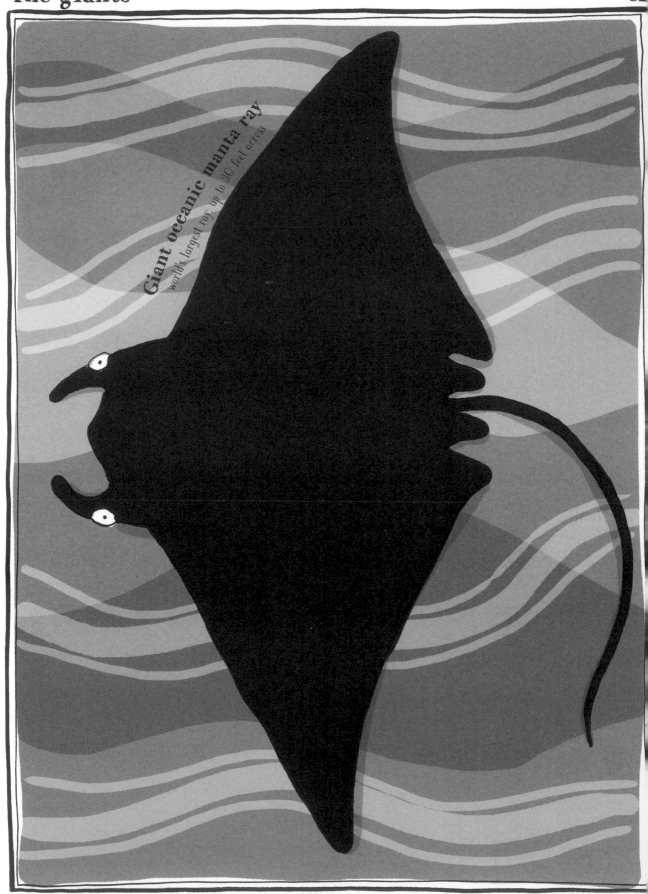

Giant oceanic manta ray
worlds largest ray, up to 30 feet across

Titan beetle
up to 6.5 inches long

Capybara
world's largest rodent: up to 4 feet long

Gorilla
world's largest primate: up to 6 feet tall

Green anaconda *up to 30 feet long*

Reticulated python up to 33 feet long

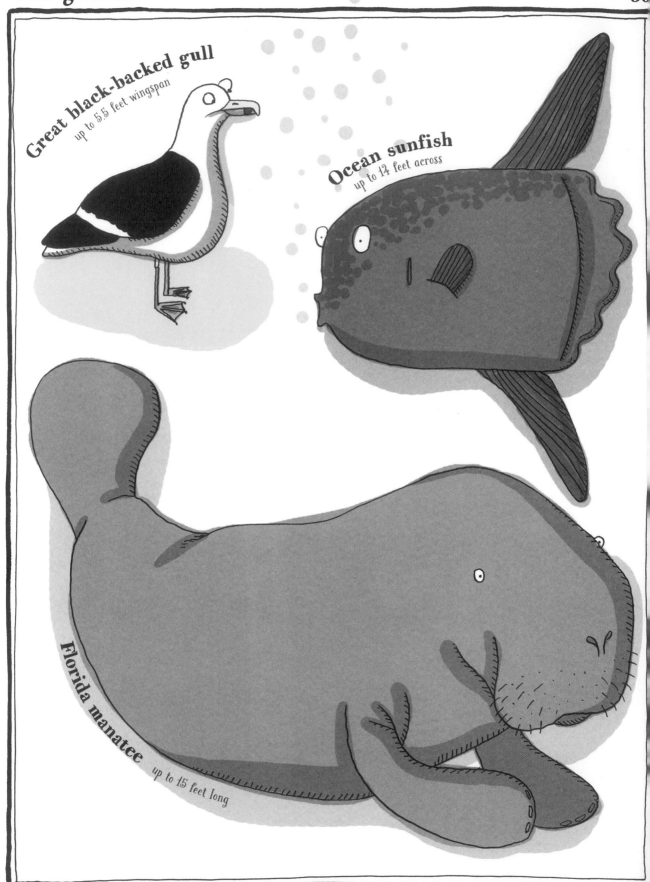

Great black-backed gull
up to 5.5 feet wingspan

Ocean sunfish
up to 14 feet across

Florida manatee
up to 15 feet long

The gladiators

Musk ox herd forms a tight circle, facing outward, for defense; bulls will sometimes charge at attackers

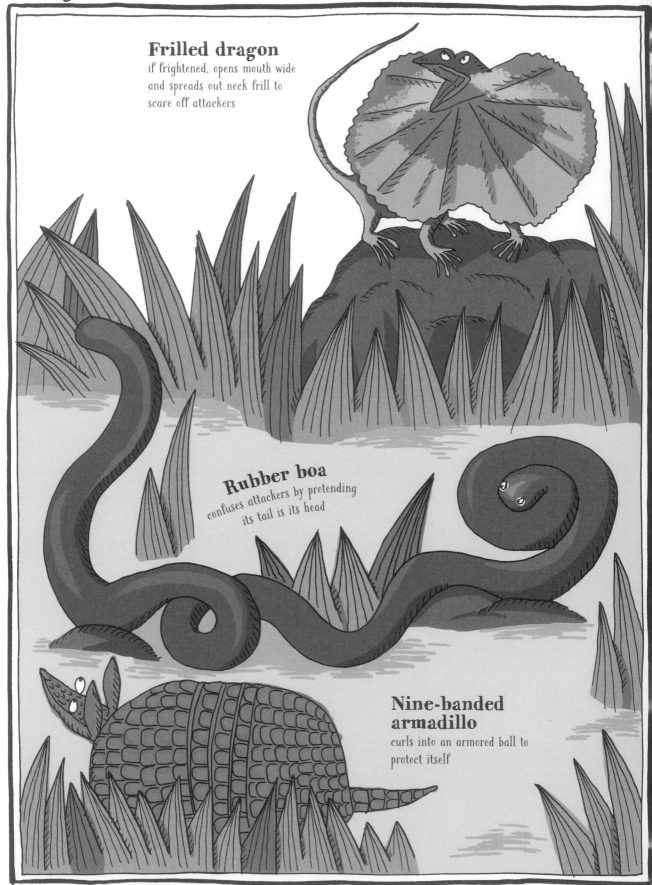

Frilled dragon
if frightened, opens mouth wide
and spreads out neck frill to
scare off attackers

Rubber boa
confuses attackers by pretending
its tail is its head

Nine-banded armadillo
curls into an armored ball to
protect itself

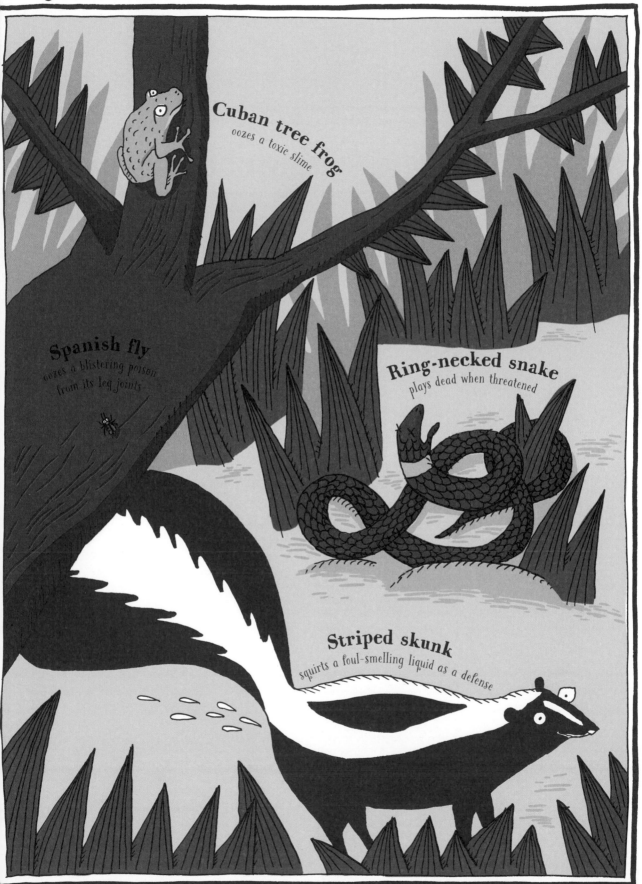

Cuban tree frog
oozes a toxic slime

Spanish fly
oozes a blistering poison
from its leg joints

Ring-necked snake
plays dead when threatened

Striped skunk
squirts a foul-smelling liquid as a defense

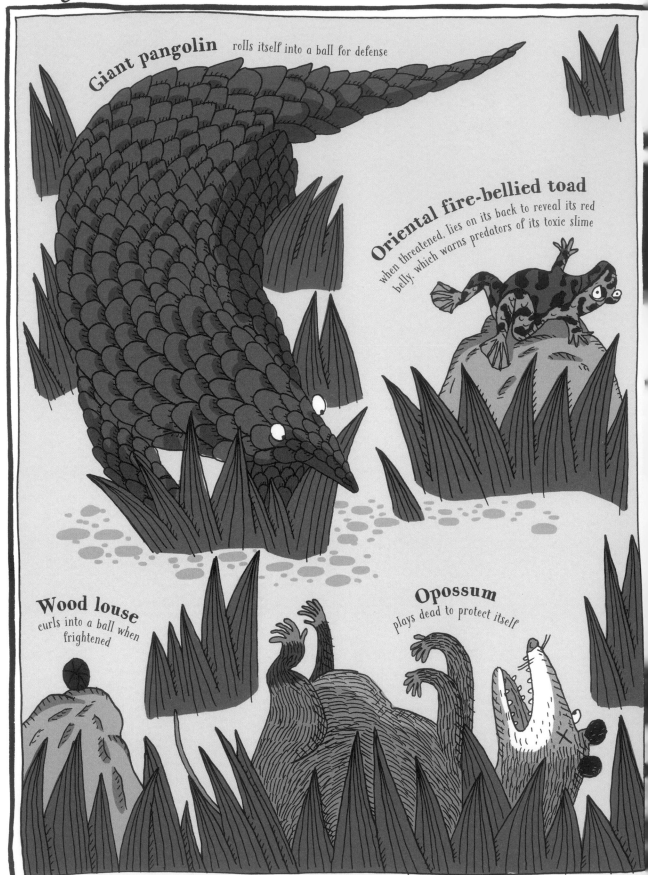

Giant pangolin rolls itself into a ball for defense

Oriental fire-bellied toad when threatened, lies on its back to reveal its red belly, which warns predators of its toxic slime

Wood louse curls into a ball when frightened

Opossum plays dead to protect itself

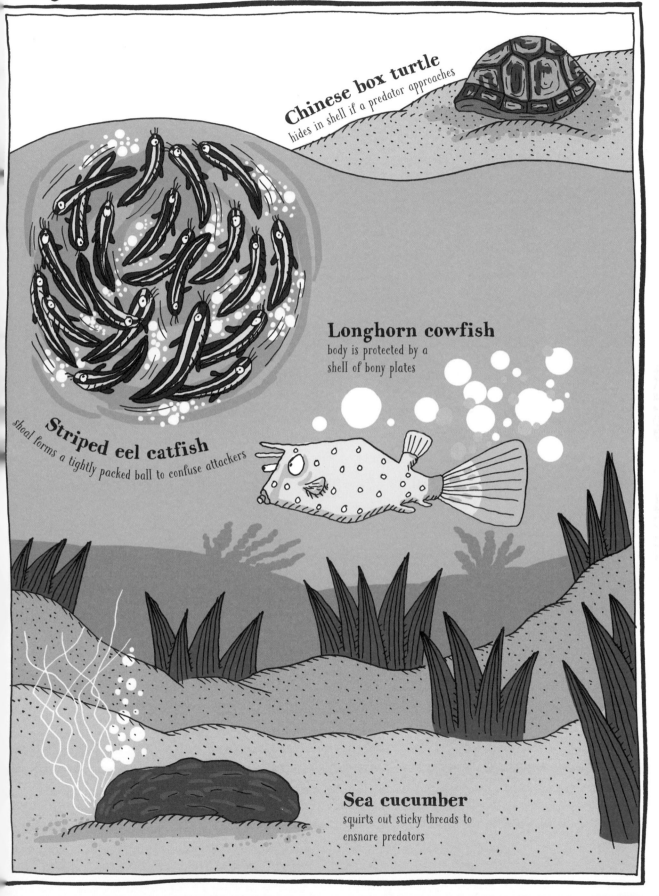

Chinese box turtle
hides in shell if a predator approaches

Longhorn cowfish
body is protected by a
shell of bony plates

Striped eel catfish
shoal forms a tightly packed ball to confuse attackers

Sea cucumber
squirts out sticky threads to
ensnare predators

The homebodies

Wild boar
remains in one territory, leaving only if food runs short

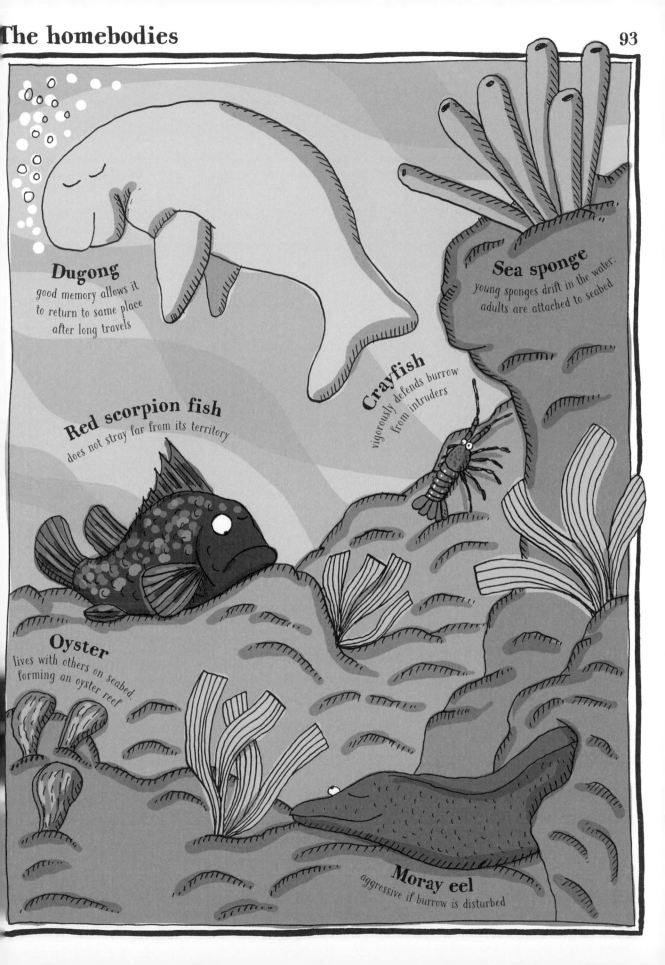

Dugong
good memory allows it
to return to same place
after long travels

Sea sponge
young sponges drift in the water,
adults are attached to seabed

Crayfish
vigorously defends burrow
from intruders

Red scorpion fish
does not stray far from its territory

Oyster
lives with others on seabed,
forming an oyster reef

Moray eel
aggressive if burrow is disturbed

Magpie
breeding pairs have territory of about 12 acres

Hermann's tortoise
strong homing instinct

Common kingfisher
very territorial; controls a stretch of river

The Lilliputians

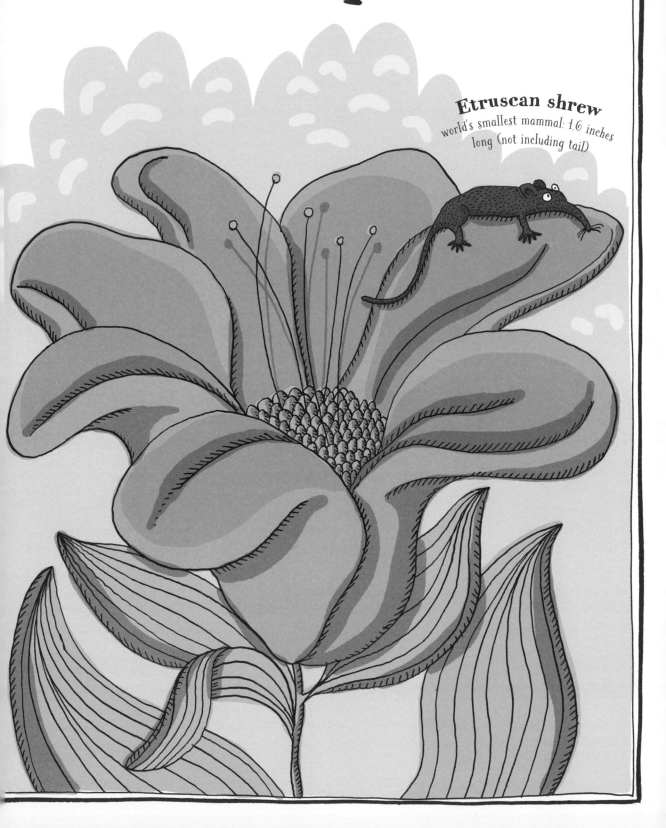

Etruscan shrew
world's smallest mammal: 1.6 inches long (not including tail)

Red panda
22 inches long
(not including tail)

**Lesser white-
fronted goose**
24 inches long

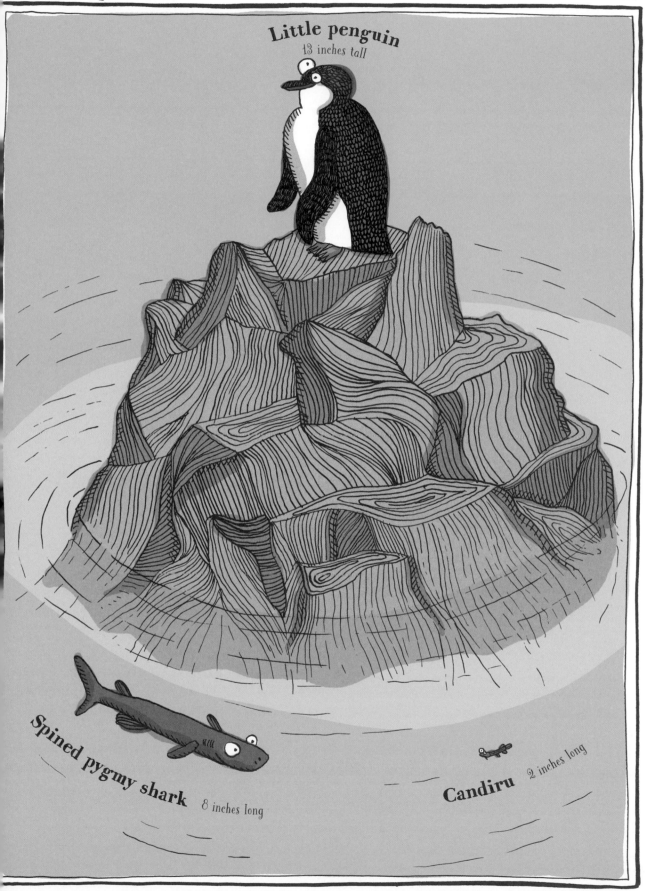

Little penguin
13 inches tall

Spined pygmy shark 8 inches long

Candiru 2 inches long

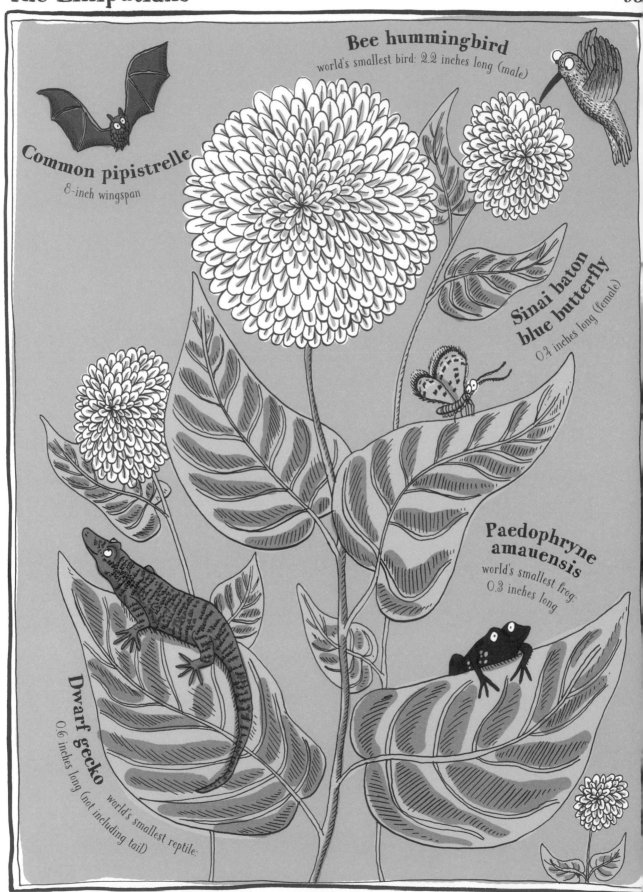

Bee hummingbird
world's smallest bird: 2.2 inches long (male)

Common pipistrelle
8-inch wingspan

Sinai baton blue butterfly
0.2 inches long (female)

Paedophryne amauensis
world's smallest frog:
0.3 inches long

Dwarf gecko
0.6 inches long (not including tail)
world's smallest reptile:

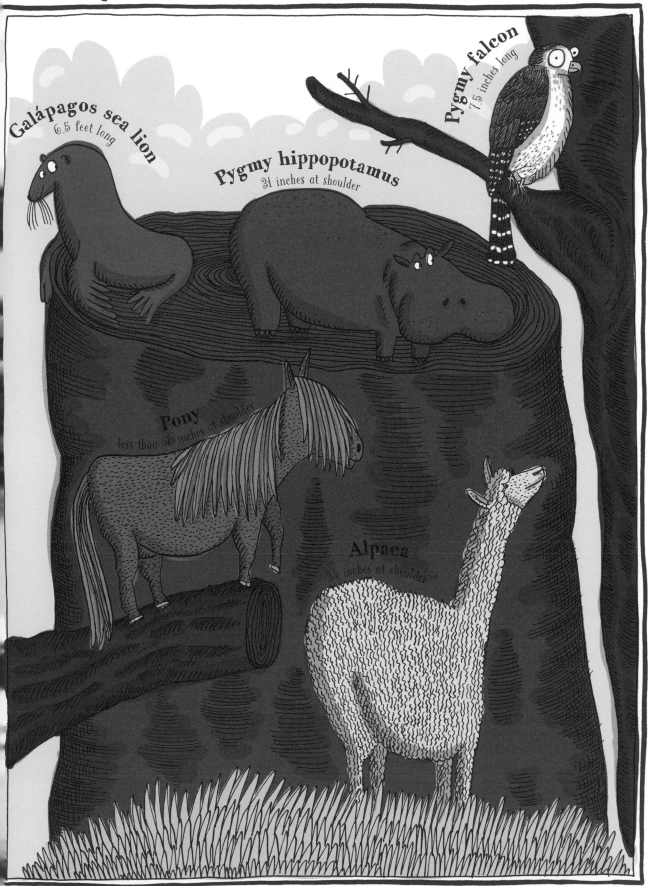

Galápagos sea lion
6.5 feet long

Pygmy hippopotamus
31 inches at shoulder

Pygmy falcon
7.5 inches long

Pony
less than 58 inches at shoulder

Alpaca
35 inches at shoulder

The long-necked

Waller's gazelle
can reach high branches
for leaves

Dromedary camel
long neck helps it reach high branches to feed

California sea lion
long, flexible neck makes it an agile swimmer

Purple heron
extends long neck to
catch fish

Mute swan
can't dive, so uses neck to reach food on lakes and riverbeds

Great egret
tucks neck in when flying

Great crested grebe
neck helps reach fish when diving underwater

Eastern long-necked turtle
neck allows it to breathe at surface while body is hidden underwater

Guanaco
skin on neck is extra-thick to protect against puma bites

Greater rhea
can easily scan for danger thanks to long neck

Giraffe weevil (male)
uses neck for fighting other males and building a nest

The long-tongued

Black woodpecker tongue = 4 inches

Okapi tongue = 14 inches

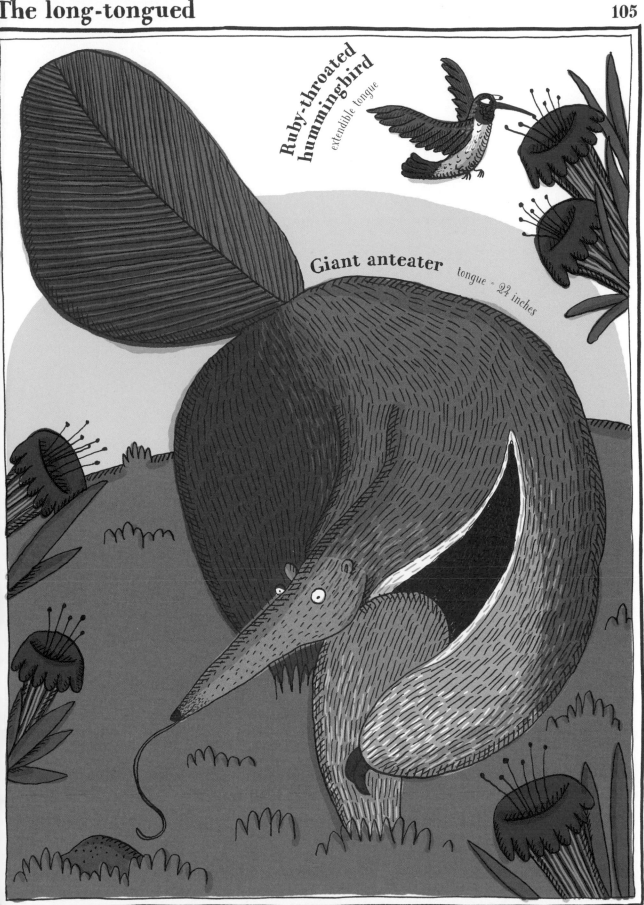

Ruby-throated hummingbird *extendible tongue*

Giant anteater *tongue = 24 inches*

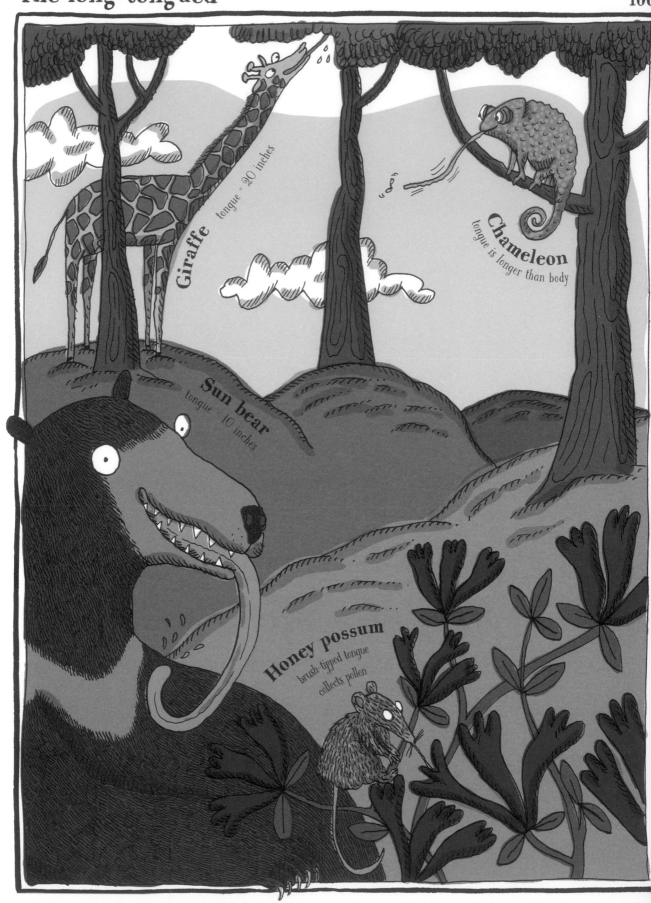

Giraffe tongue = 20 inches

Chameleon tongue is longer than body

Sun bear tongue 10 inches

Honey possum brush-tipped tongue collects pollen

The masters of camouflage

Bush cricket

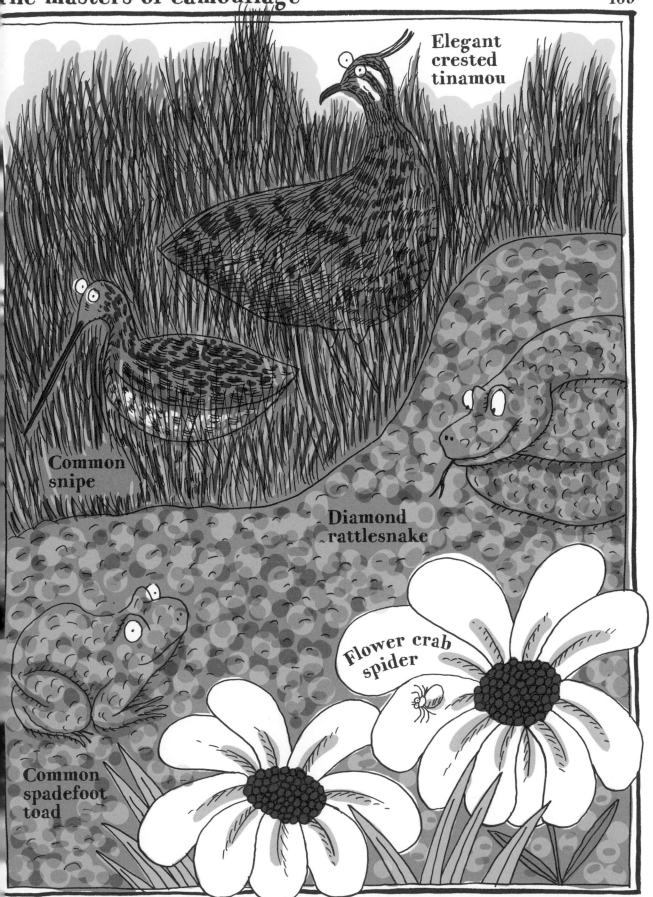

Elegant crested tinamou

Common snipe

Diamond rattlesnake

Common spadefoot toad

Flower crab spider

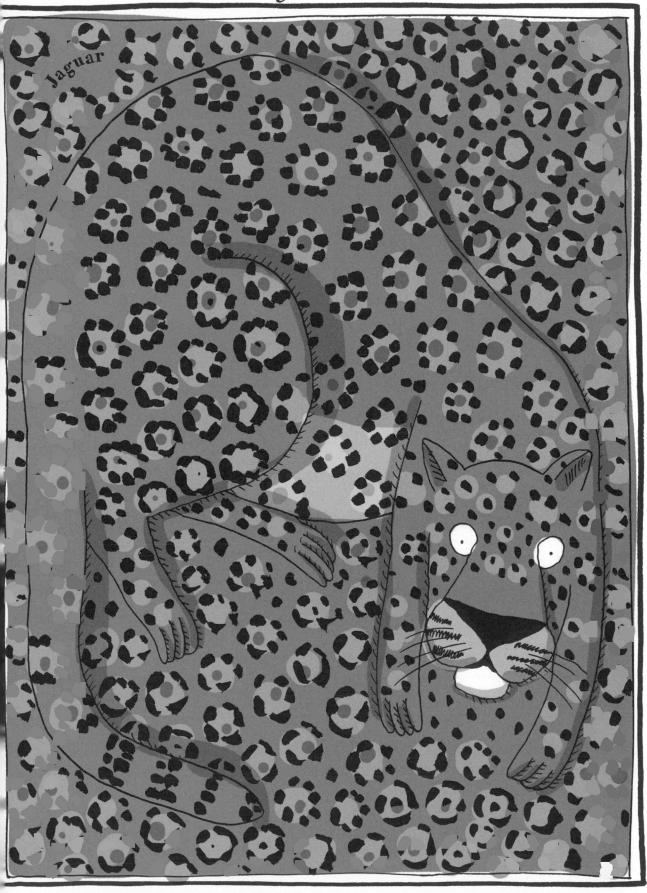

Jaguar

The mountaineers

Bearded vulture
seen on Mt Everest at 24,600 feet

Griffon vulture
nests among steep cliffs

Mouflon
wild sheep; horns can grow 33 inches long

Alpine chough
thought to build nest higher than any other bird

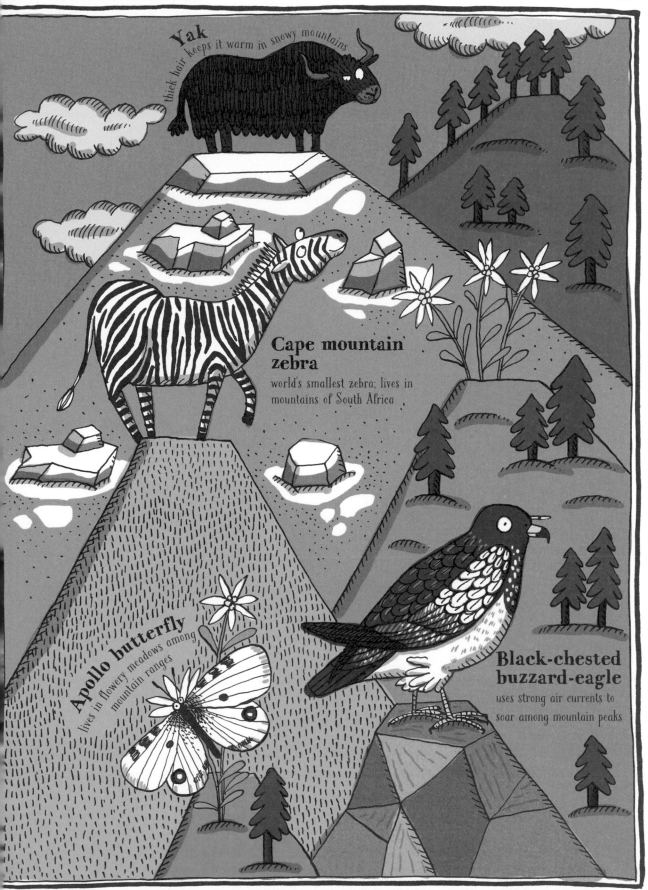

Yak
thick hair keeps it warm in snowy mountains

Cape mountain zebra
world's smallest zebra; lives in mountains of South Africa

Apollo butterfly
lives in flowery meadows among mountain ranges

Black-chested buzzard-eagle
uses strong air currents to soar among mountain peaks

Andean condor
huge 10-foot wingspan; glides on air currents

Rock ptarmigan
molts to change color so blends in as seasons turn

Marmot
hibernates in group burrow during freezing winter

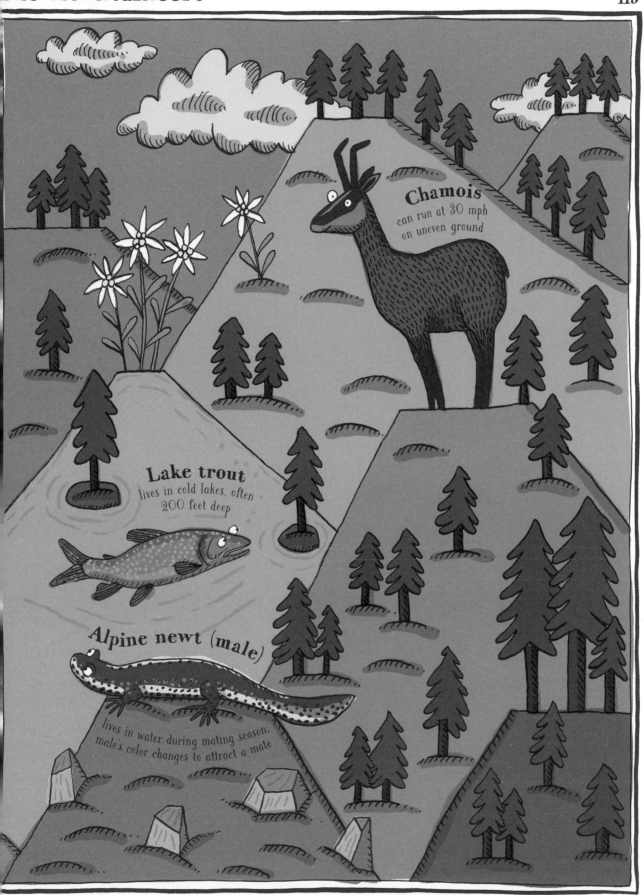

Chamois
can run at 30 mph
on uneven ground

Lake trout
lives in cold lakes, often
200 feet deep

Alpine newt (male)

lives in water during mating season,
male's color changes to attract a mate

The munch-it-uppers

Tiger hunts in darkness with night vision six times better than humans'

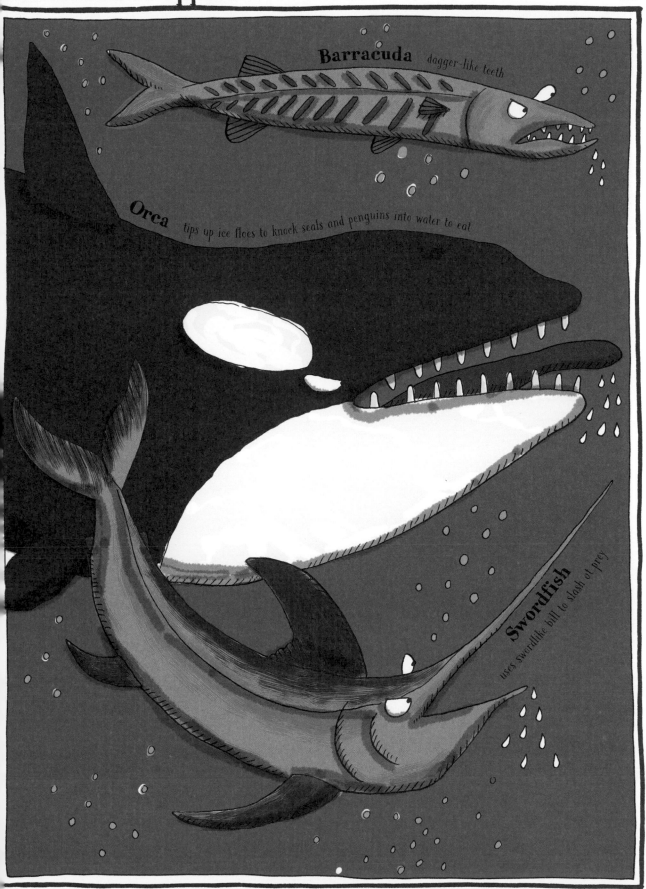

Barracuda *dagger-like teeth*

Orca *tips up ice floes to knock seals and penguins into water to eat*

Swordfish *uses swordlike bill to slash at prey*

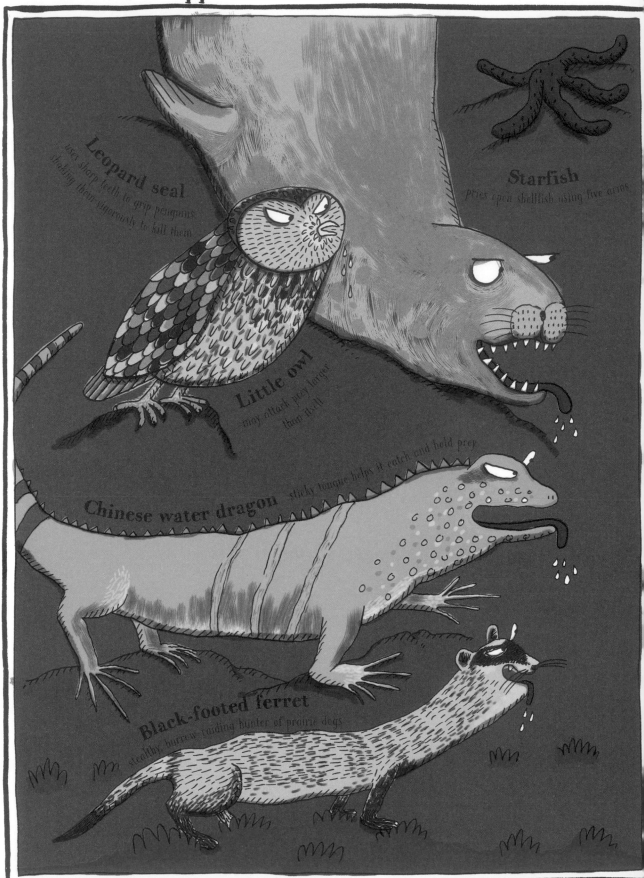

Leopard seal
uses sharp teeth to grip penguins, shaking them vigorously to kill them

Starfish
pries open shellfish using five arms

Little owl
may attack prey larger than itself

Chinese water dragon sticky tongue helps it catch and hold prey

Black-footed ferret
stealthy burrow-raiding hunter of prairie dogs

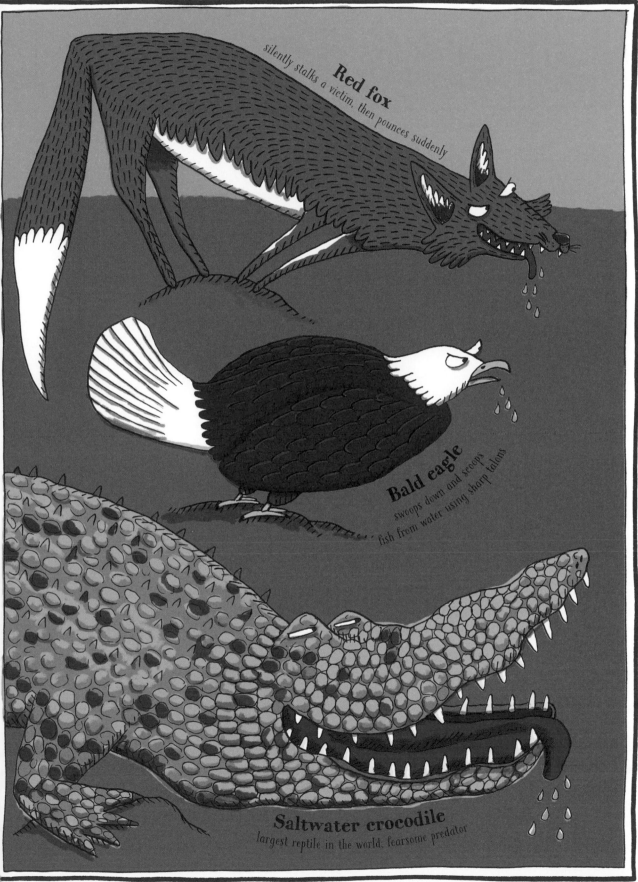

Red fox
silently stalks a victim, then pounces suddenly

Bald eagle
swoops down and scoops
fish from water using sharp talons

Saltwater crocodile
largest reptile in the world, fearsome predator

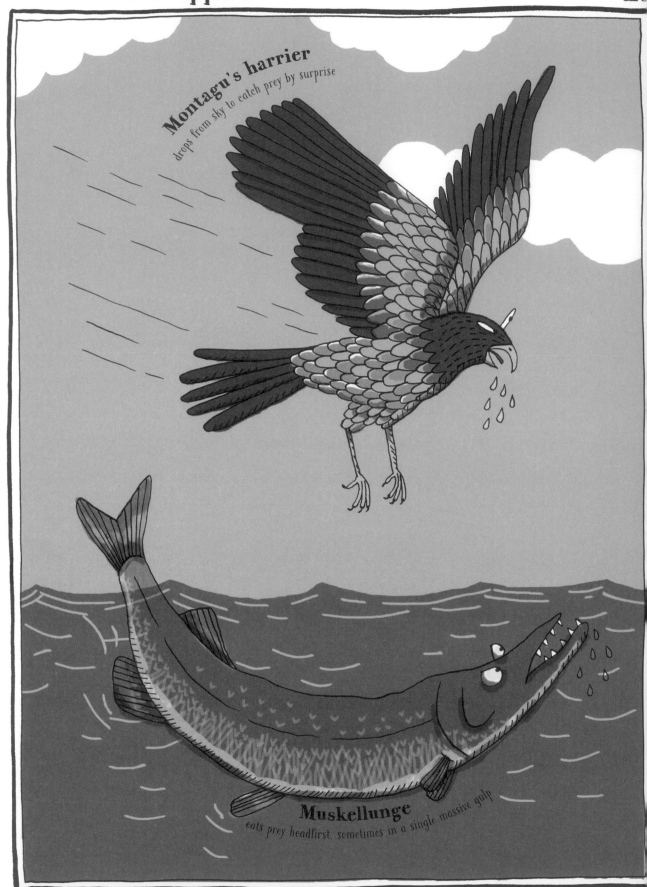

Montagu's harrier
drops from sky to catch prey by surprise

Muskellunge
eats prey headfirst, sometimes in a single massive gulp

The mythical

Pegasus

Yeti

Dahu
mountain goat with legs on
one side shorter than other side

Dragon

Snouter
small mammal that uses nose
for everything, including jumping
and fishing

Griffin

Lernaean Hydra

Baku
eater of nightmares

The night owls

Eurasian eagle-owl
night vision, powerful hearing, and silent
flight make it a deadly predator

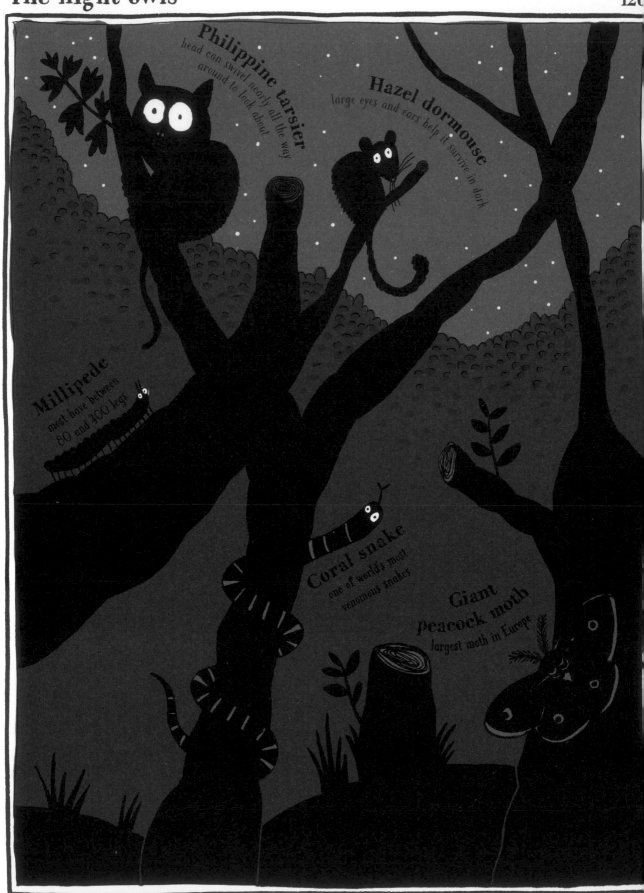

Philippine tarsier
head can swivel nearly all the way around to look about

Hazel dormouse
large eyes and ears help it survive in dark

Millipede
most have between 80 and 300 legs

Coral snake
one of world's most venomous snakes

Giant peacock moth
largest moth in Europe

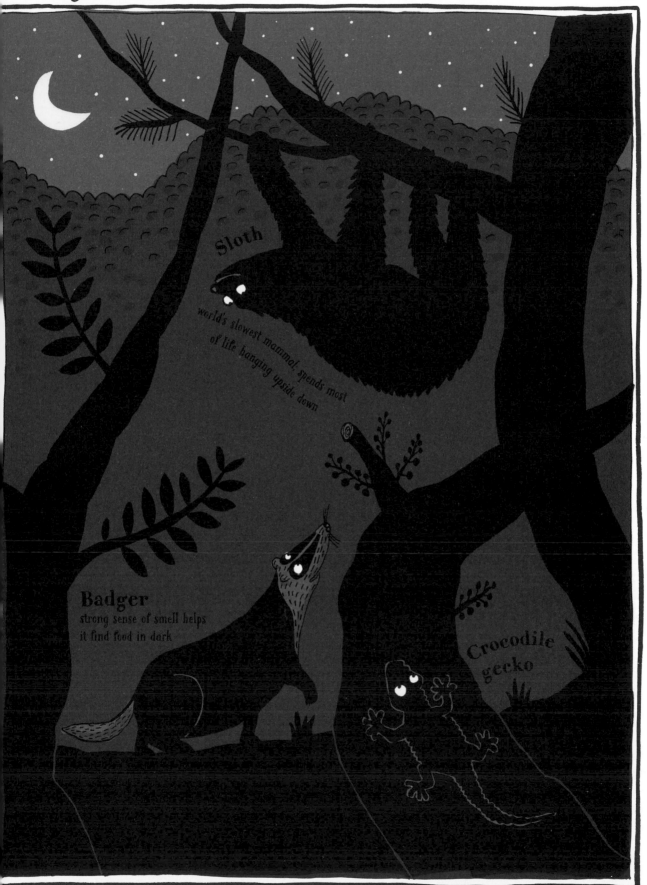

Sloth
world's slowest mammal, spends most of life hanging upside down

Badger
strong sense of smell helps it find food in dark

Crocodile gecko

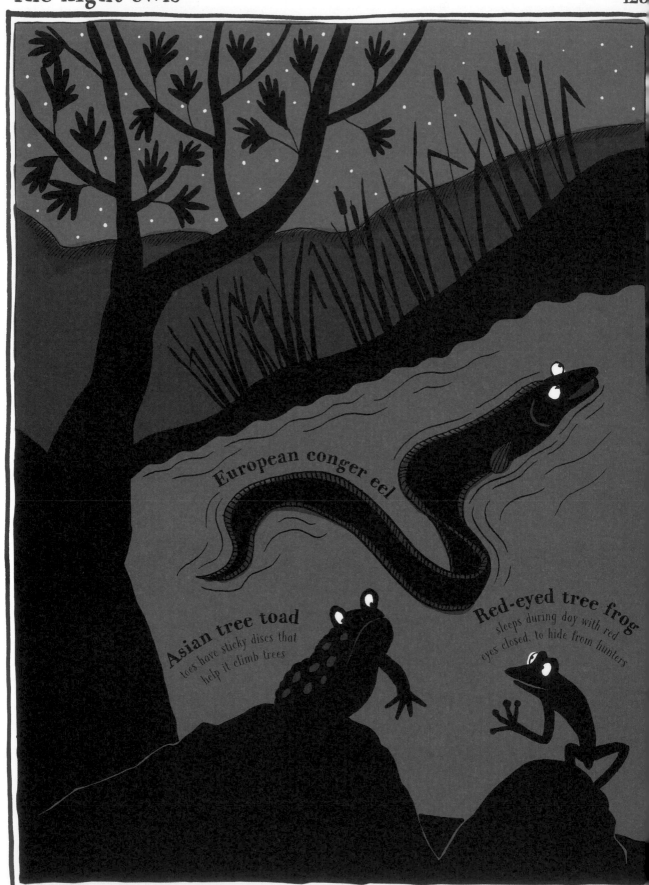

European conger eel

Asian tree toad
toes have sticky discs that help it climb trees

Red-eyed tree frog
sleeps during day with red eyes closed, to hide from hunters

Brazilian tapir
hides in water to avoid
attackers, using snout as a
snorkel

Stone loach

Squirrelfish

Kiwi
shy, flightless bird, lives only in New Zealand

Spanish moon moth

Barn owl

excellent hearing helps it find prey even in pitch-dark, one ear is slightly higher than other, helping owl pinpoint sounds

The pack animals

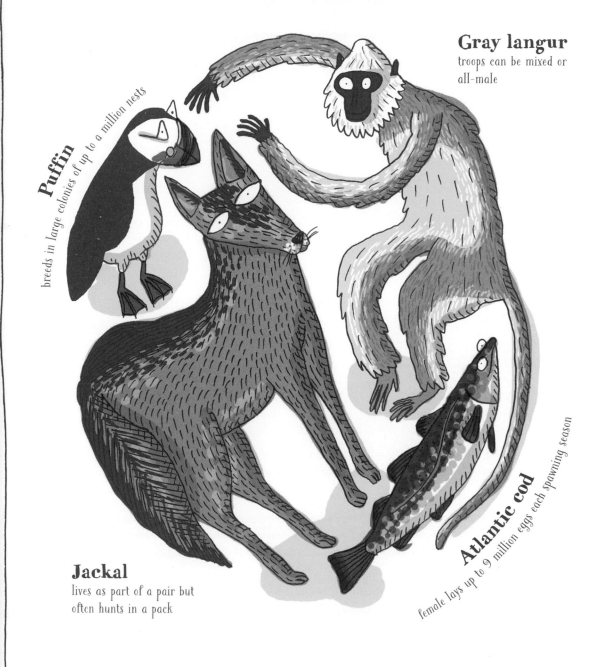

Gray langur
troops can be mixed or all-male

Puffin
breeds in large colonies of up to a million nests

Jackal
lives as part of a pair but often hunts in a pack

Atlantic cod
female lays up to 9 million eggs each spawning season

The pack animals

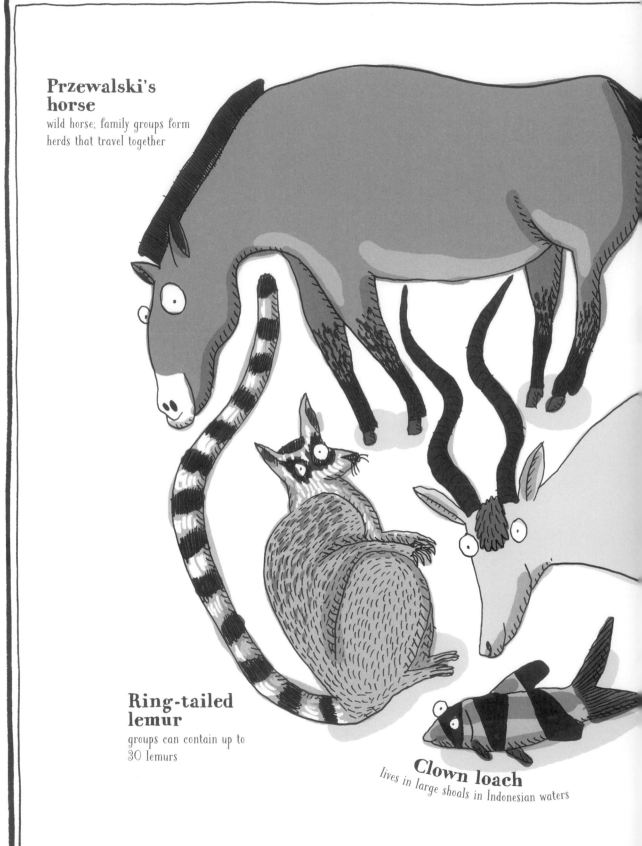

Przewalski's horse
wild horse; family groups form herds that travel together

Ring-tailed lemur
groups can contain up to 30 lemurs

Clown loach
lives in large shoals in Indonesian waters

Hippopotamus
groups, called pods, can contain 100 hippos

European honeybee
lives in a hive of up to 80,000

Addax
lives in a herd of up to 20

Bearded dragon
gathers in groups to feed or sunbathe

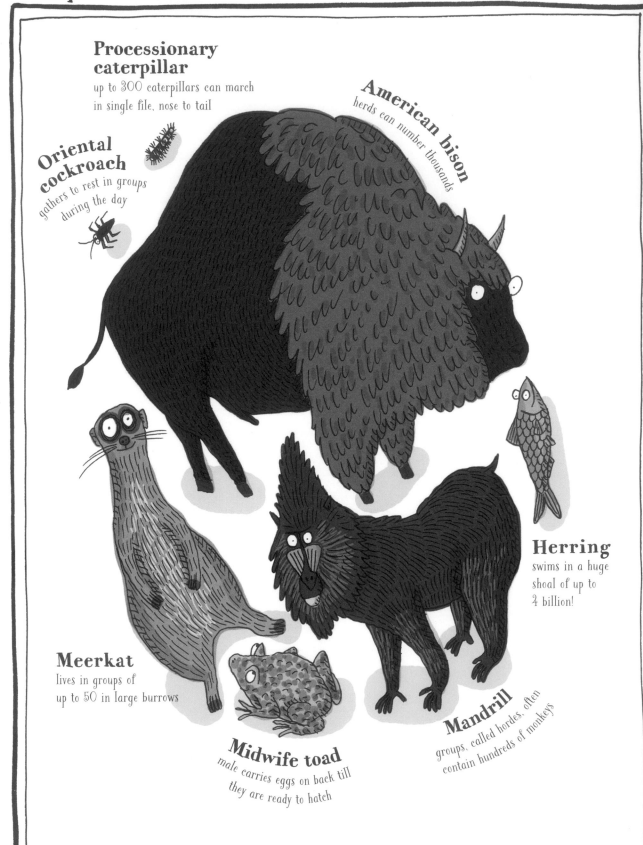

Processionary caterpillar
up to 300 caterpillars can march in single file, nose to tail

American bison
herds can number thousands

Oriental cockroach
gathers to rest in groups during the day

Herring
swims in a huge shoal of up to ½ billion!

Meerkat
lives in groups of up to 50 in large burrows

Midwife toad
male carries eggs on back till they are ready to hatch

Mandrill
groups, called hordes, often contain hundreds of monkeys

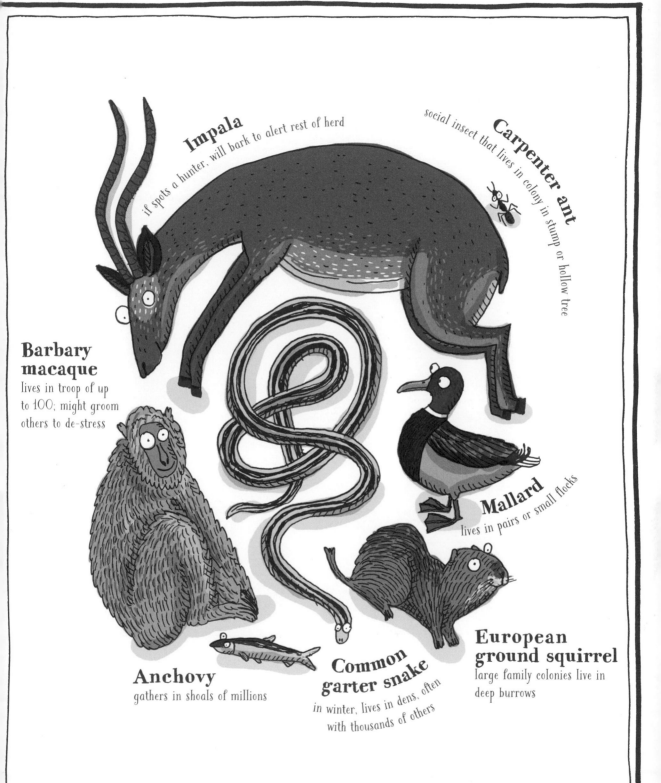

Impala
if spots a hunter, will bark to alert rest of herd

Carpenter ant
social insect that lives in colony in stump or hollow tree

Barbary macaque
lives in troop of up to 100; might groom others to de-stress

Mallard
lives in pairs or small flocks

Anchovy
gathers in shoals of millions

Common garter snake
in winter, lives in dens, often with thousands of others

European ground squirrel
large family colonies live in deep burrows

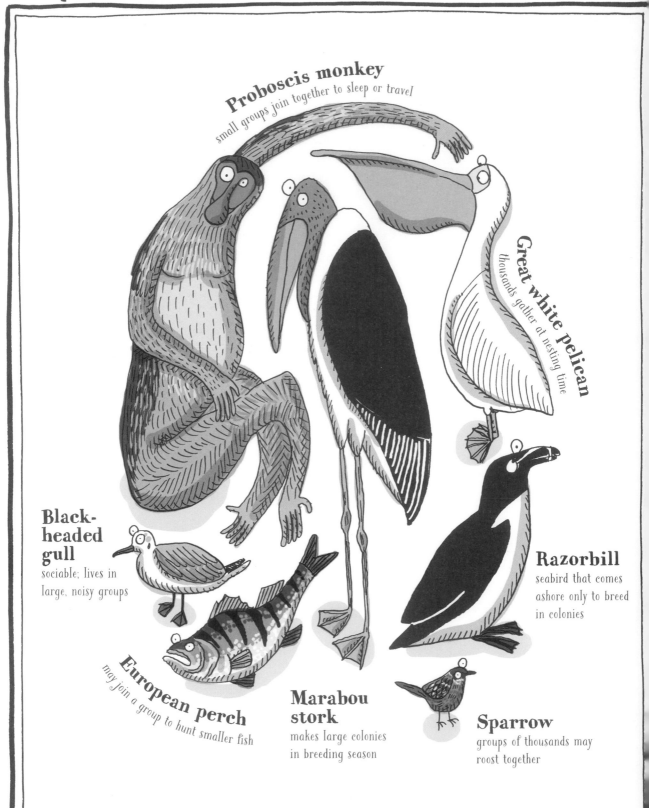

Proboscis monkey
small groups join together to sleep or travel

Great white pelican
thousands gather at nesting time

Black-headed gull
sociable; lives in large, noisy groups

Razorbill
seabird that comes ashore only to breed in colonies

European perch
may join a group to hunt smaller fish

Marabou stork
makes large colonies in breeding season

Sparrow
groups of thousands may roost together

The poisonous

Bushmaster
venomous bite

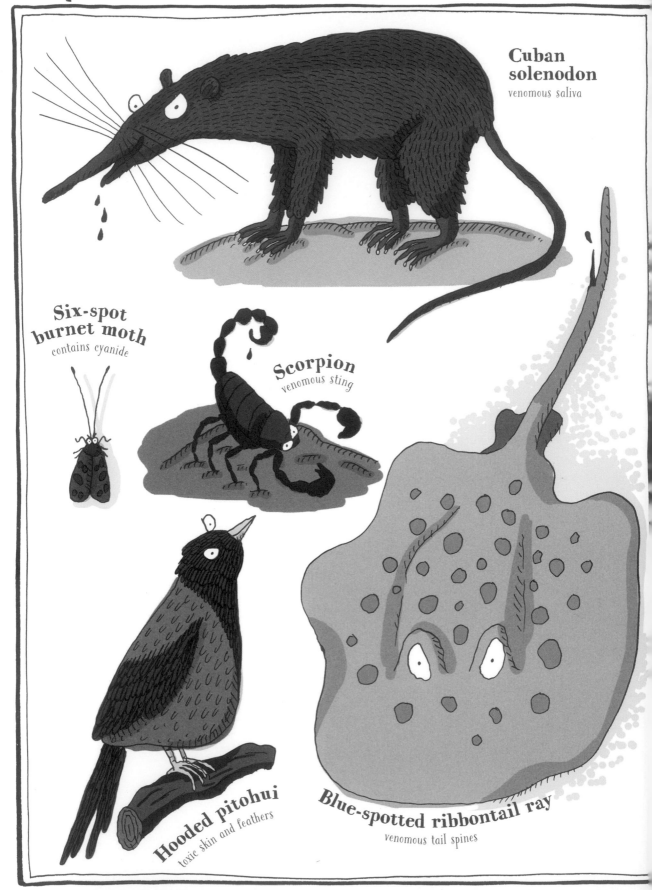

Cuban solenodon
venomous saliva

Six-spot burnet moth
contains cyanide

Scorpion
venomous sting

Hooded pitohui
toxic skin and feathers

Blue-spotted ribbontail ray
venomous tail spines

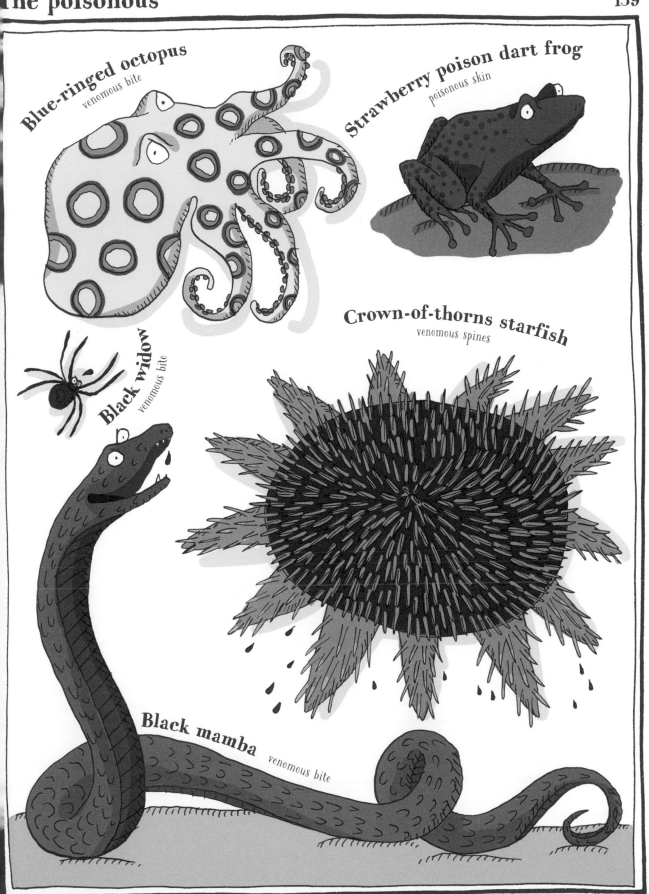

Blue-ringed octopus venomous bite

Strawberry poison dart frog poisonous skin

Crown-of-thorns starfish venomous spines

Black widow venomous bite

Black mamba venomous bite

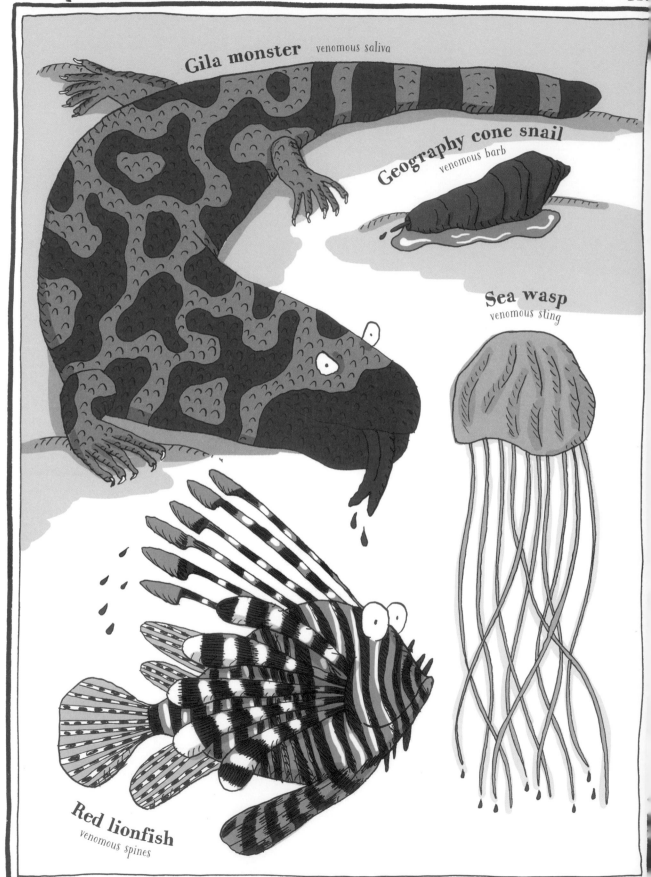

Gila monster venomous saliva

Geography cone snail venomous barb

Sea wasp venomous sting

Red lionfish venomous spines

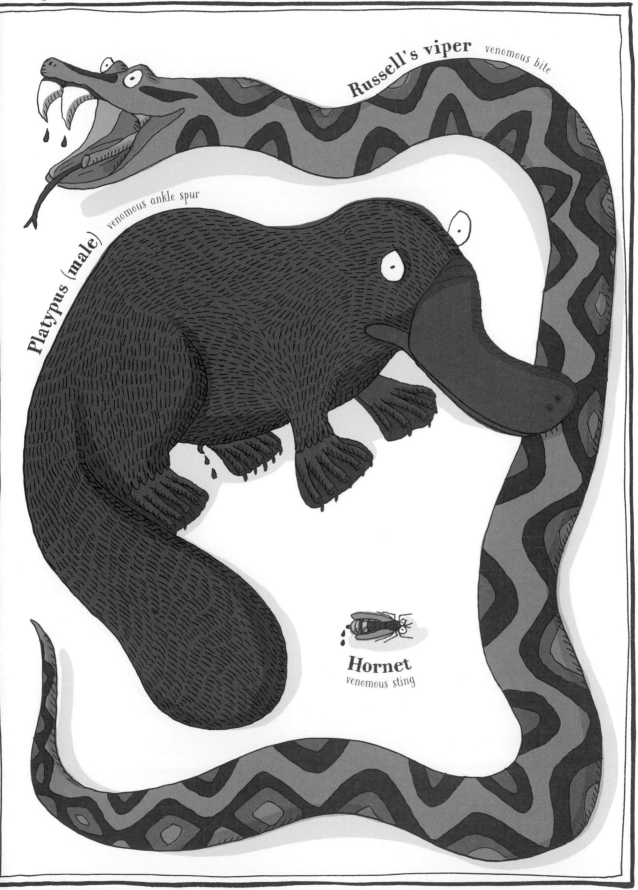

Russell's viper *venomous bite*

Platypus (male) *venomous ankle spur*

Hornet
venomous sting

The pretty-in-pinks

Pig

Earthworm

Elephant hawk moth

Roseate spoonbill

Greater flamingo

Amazon river dolphin

The prickly ones

Spiny anteater
spiky body; some even have spines on tongue to snare prey

European hedgehog
if afraid, will curl into a ball with 6,000 spines sticking out

Armadillo lizard
can put tail in mouth and roll into a prickly ball

Bay shrimp
has a spiky horn above eyes

Crested porcupine
has tiny barbs on end of quills
that stick into flesh, making
them hard to remove

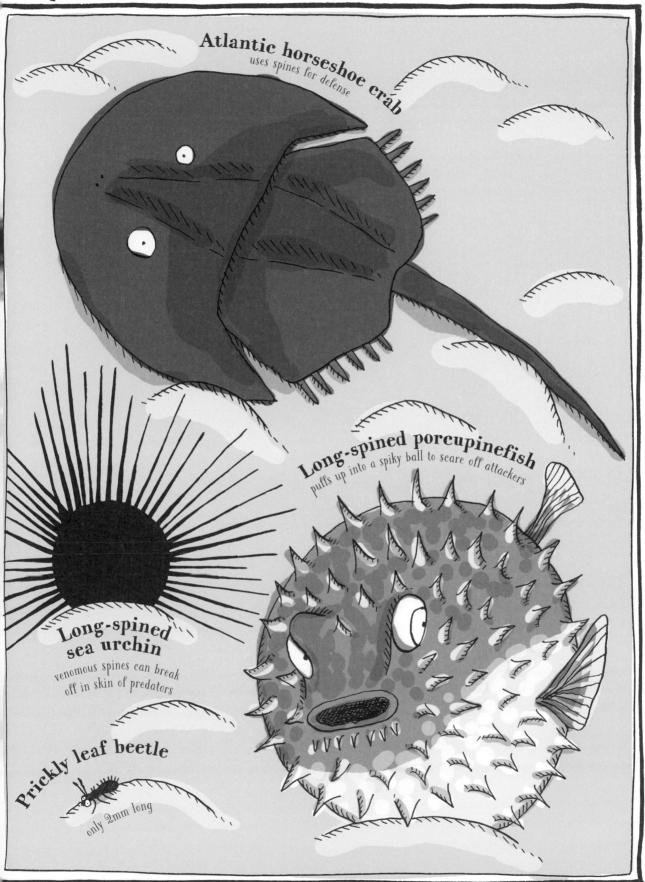

Atlantic horseshoe crab
uses spines for defense

Long-spined porcupinefish
puffs up into a spiky ball to scare off attackers

Long-spined sea urchin
venomous spines can break off in skin of predators

Prickly leaf beetle
only 2mm long

The prickly ones

Horned desert viper — horns fold back to give snake smoother shape for burrowing

Horned lizard — puffs up and sticks out spikes to scare off attackers; can also squirt blood from eyes!

The redheads

Milk snake

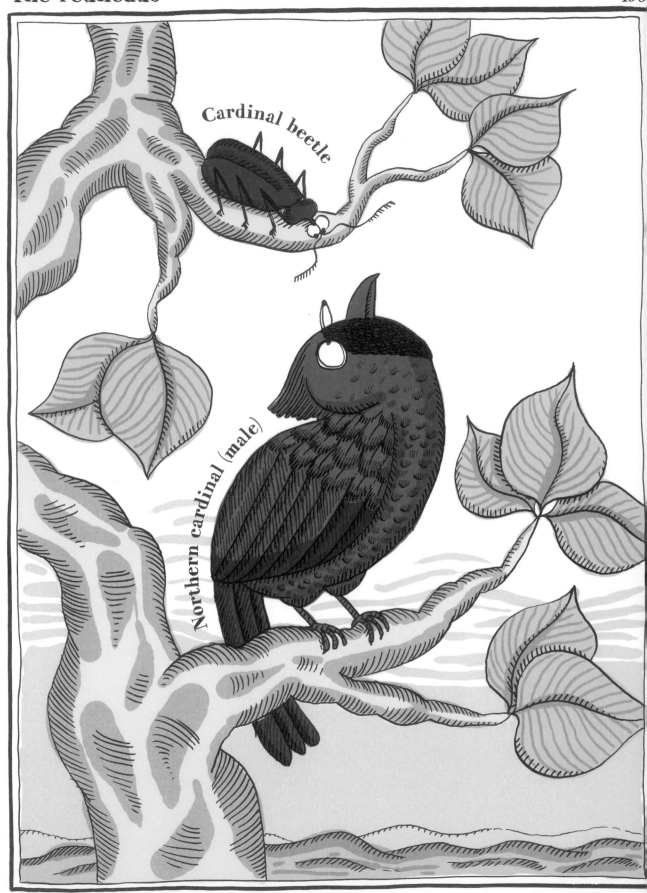

Cardinal beetle

Northern cardinal (male)

Crimson rosella

Scarlet tanager

Vermilion flycatcher

Poplar leaf beetle

Tomato frog

Orange roughy

Red weevil

Scarlet ibis

Firebug

Red salamander

The regal

Lion

Emperor scorpion

Golden eagle

Emperor angelfish

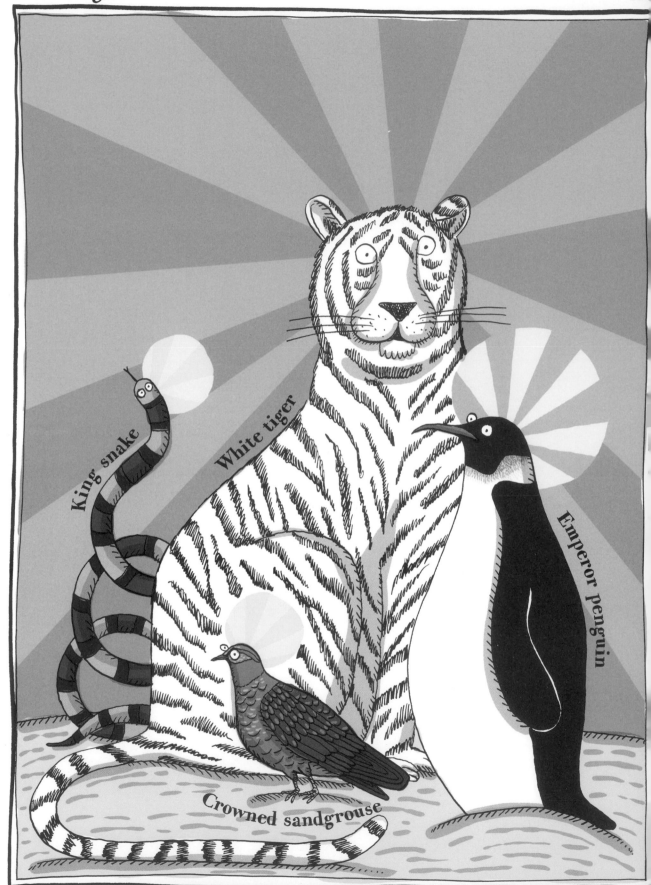

King snake

White tiger

Emperor penguin

Crowned sandgrouse

The show-offs

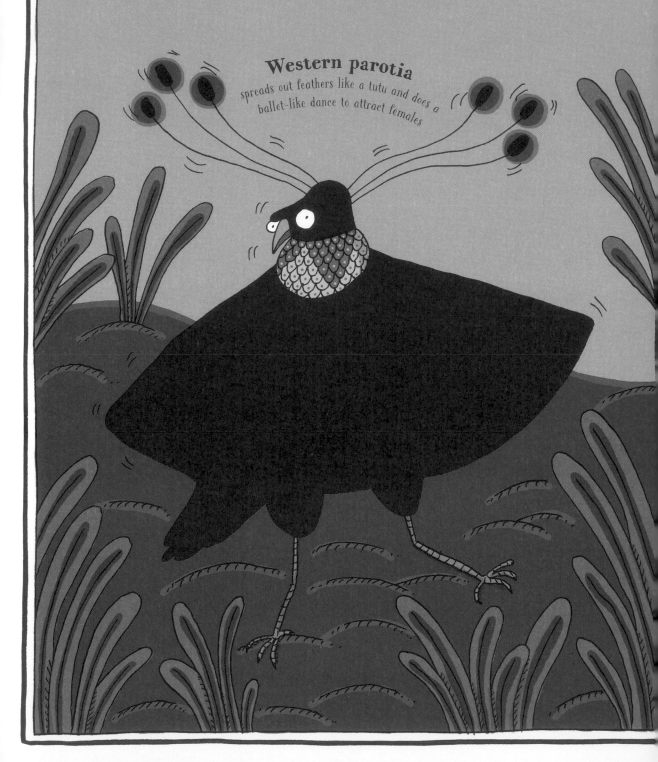

Western parotia
spreads out feathers like a tutu and does a
ballet-like dance to attract females

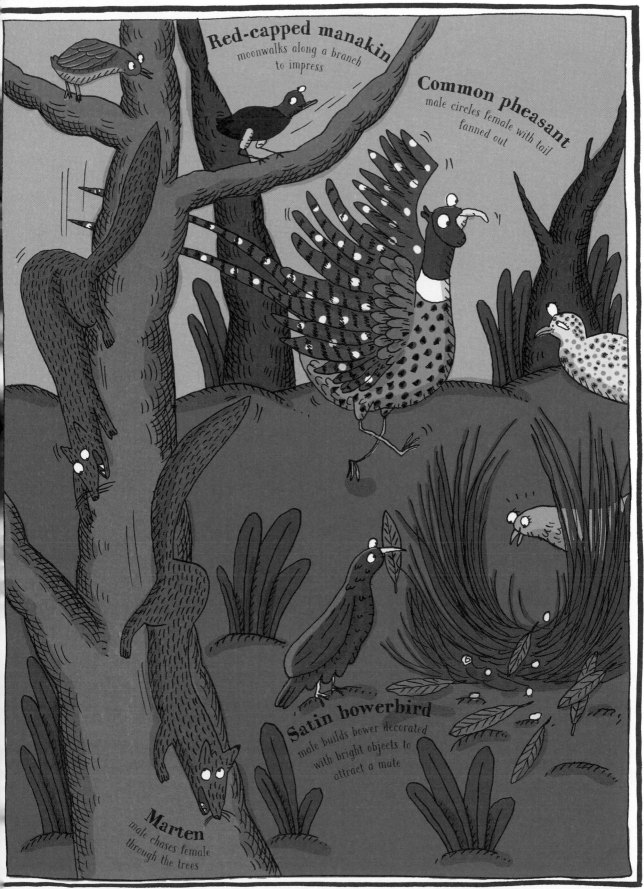

Red-capped manakin
moonwalks along a branch
to impress

Common pheasant
male circles female with tail
fanned out

Satin bowerbird
male builds bower decorated
with bright objects to
attract a mate

Marten
male chases female
through the trees

Red deer

stag bellows to warn off other males and attract females

Wood grouse
makes clicking, popping, scraping
sounds as part of mating ritual

Superb lyrebird
male fans tail, dances, and sings
to impress a mate

Magnificent frigate bird
male puffs up red throat-pouch like a balloon

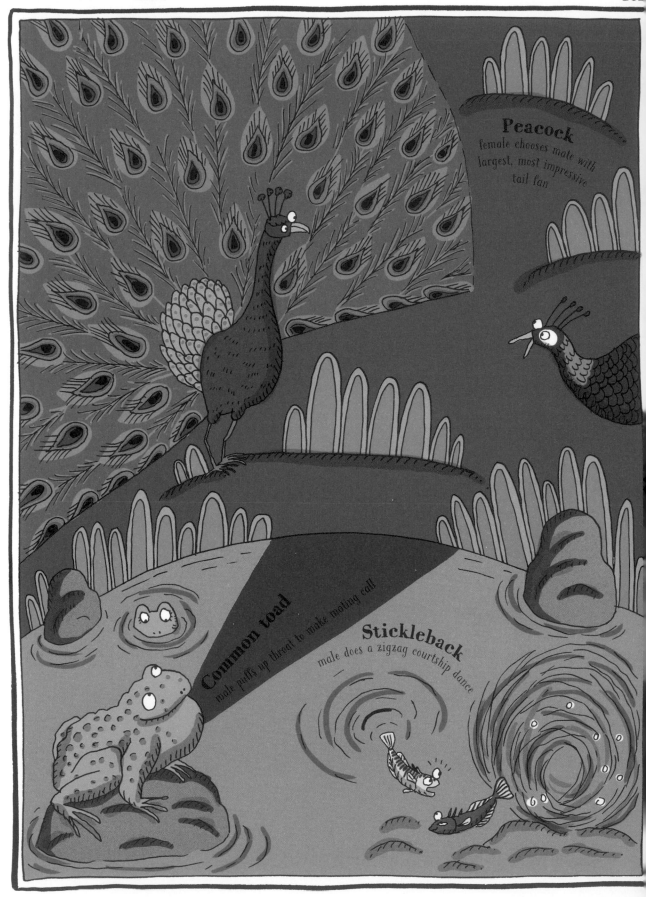

Peacock
female chooses mate with largest, most impressive tail fan

Common toad
male puffs up throat to make mating call

Stickleback
male does a zigzag courtship dance

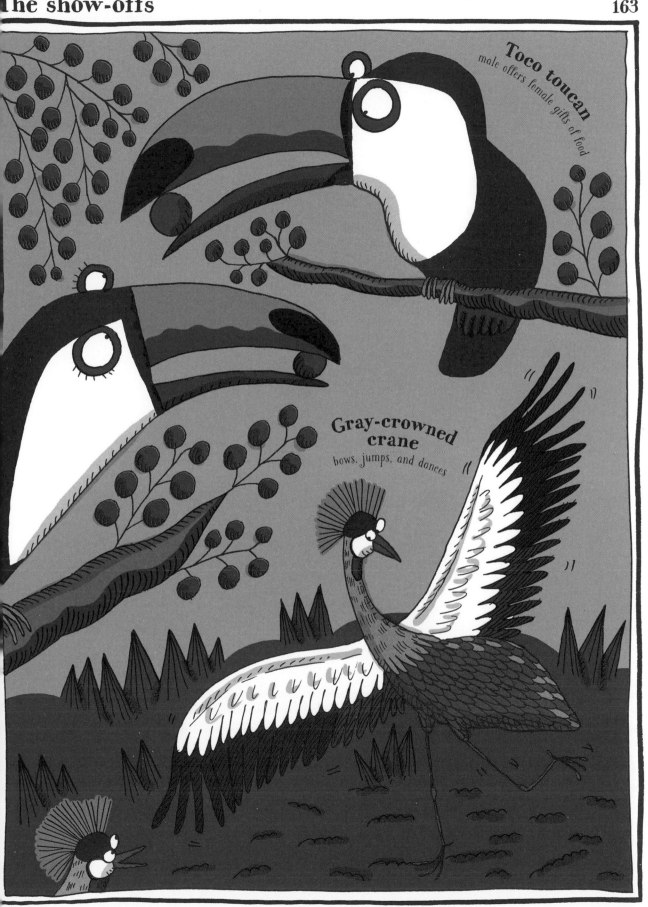

Toco toucan
male offers female gifts of food

Gray-crowned crane
bows, jumps, and dances

The snowy-whites

Polar bear

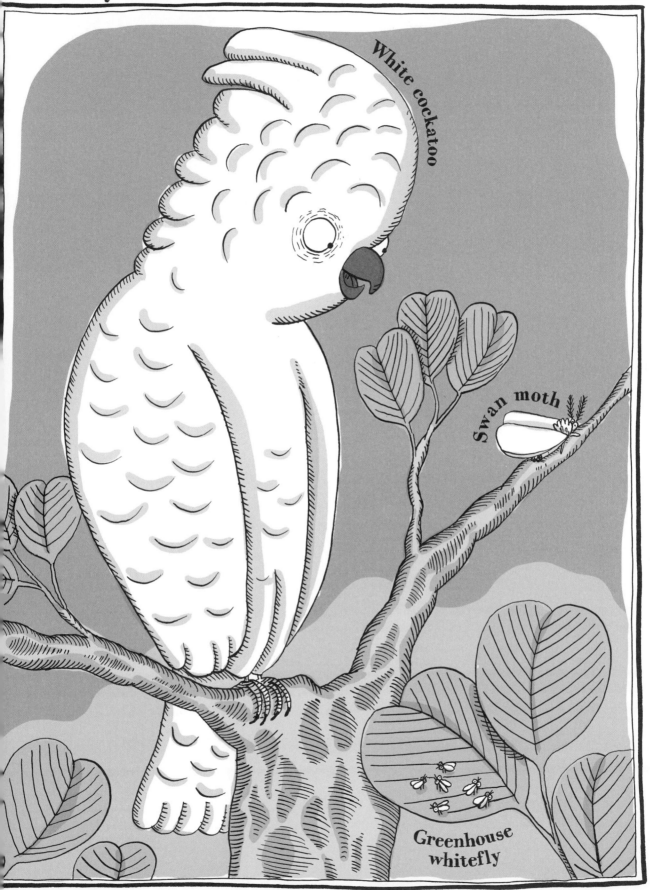

White cockatoo

Swan moth

Greenhouse whitefly

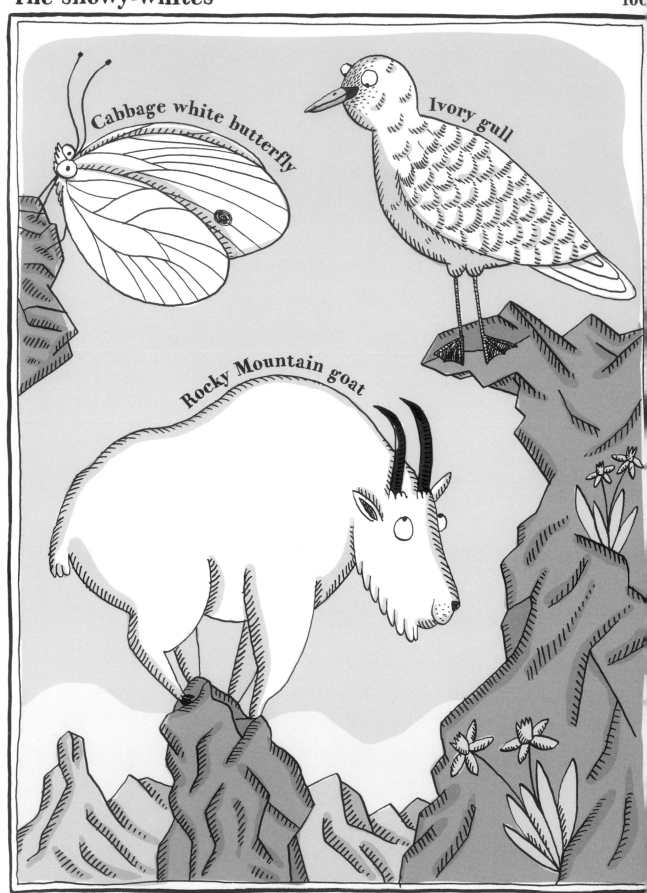

Cabbage white butterfly

Ivory gull

Rocky Mountain goat

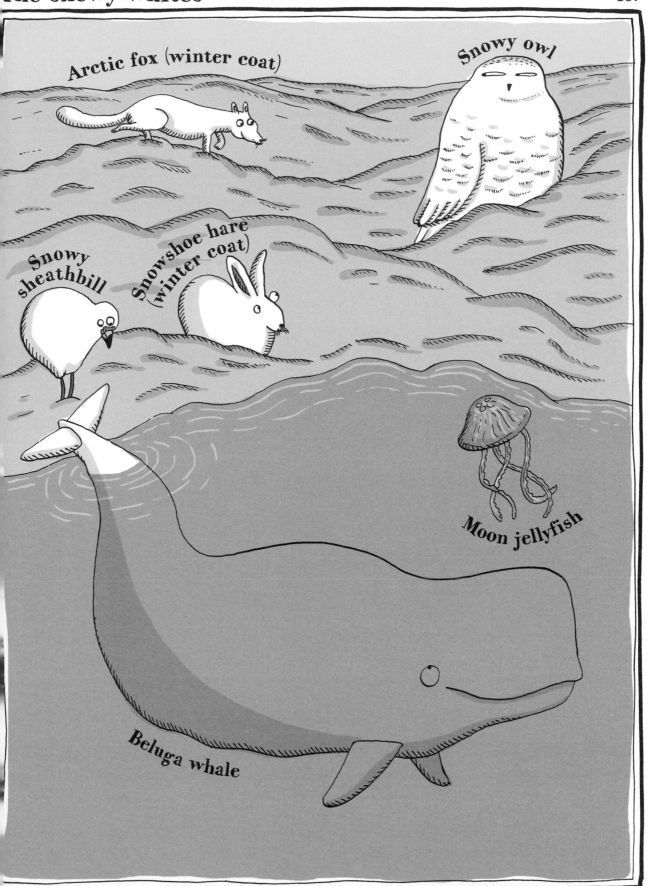

Arctic fox (winter coat)

Snowy owl

Snowy sheathbill

Snowshoe hare (winter coat)

Moon jellyfish

Beluga whale

The solitary

Nile monitor

Black vulture

Brown bear

Smooth hammerhead

Giant grouper

Praying mantis

Mole

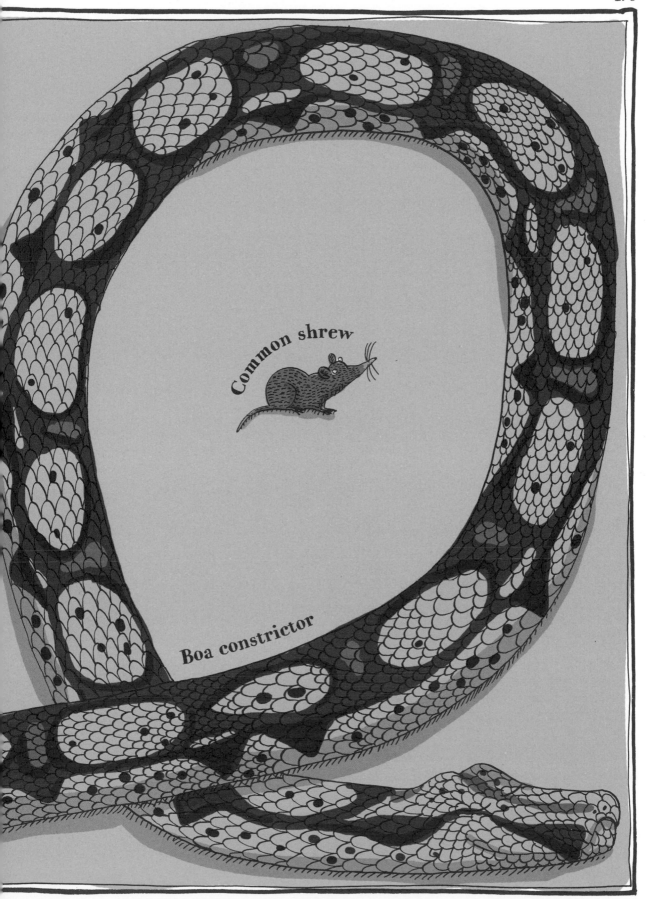

Common shrew

Boa constrictor

Siamese fighting fish

Galápagos giant tortoise

Lobster

The spotted

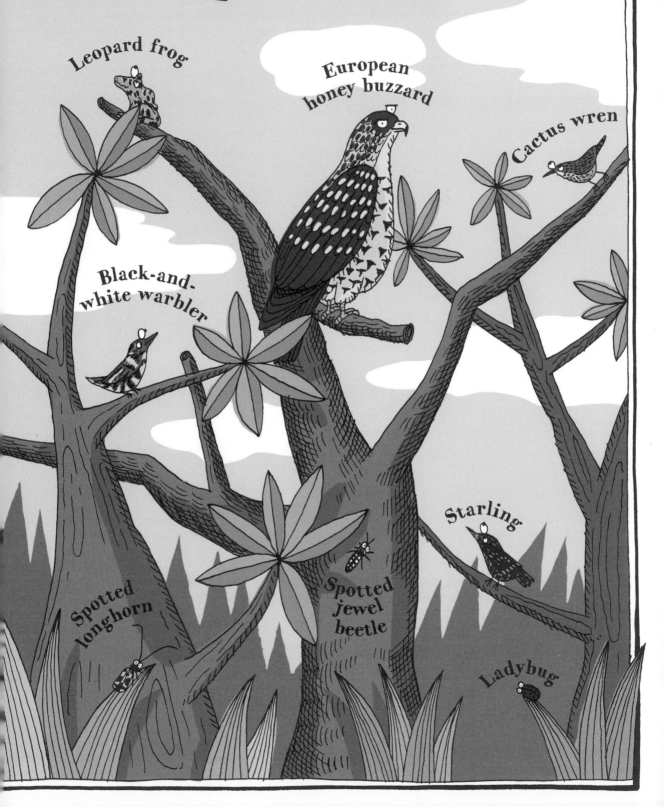

Leopard frog

European honey buzzard

Cactus wren

Black-and-white warbler

Spotted longhorn

Spotted jewel beetle

Starling

Ladybug

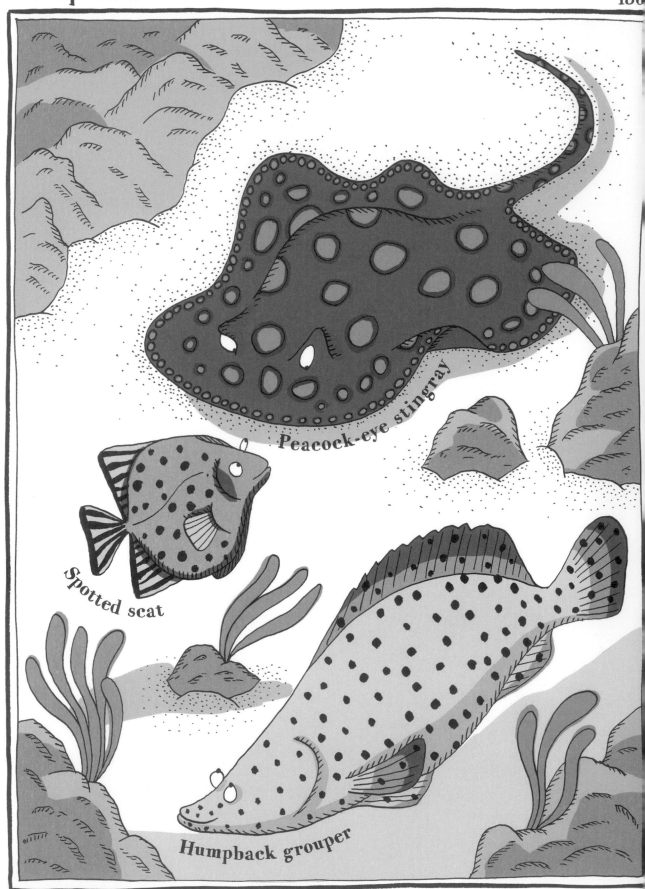

Peacock-eye stingray

Spotted scat

Humpback grouper

Fallow deer

Tiger salamander

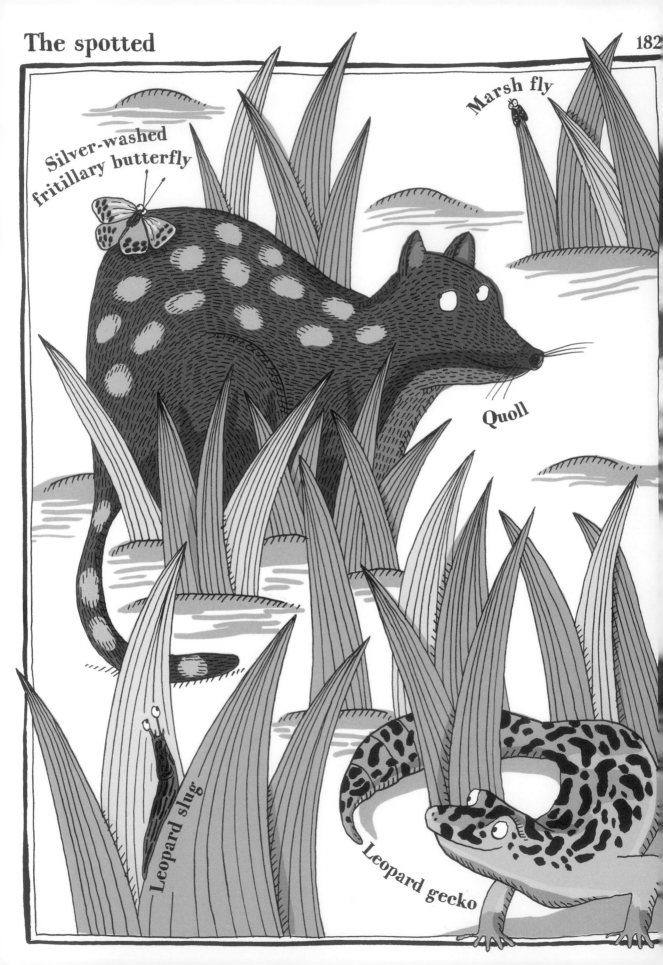

Marsh fly

Silver-washed
fritillary butterfly

Quoll

Leopard slug

Leopard gecko

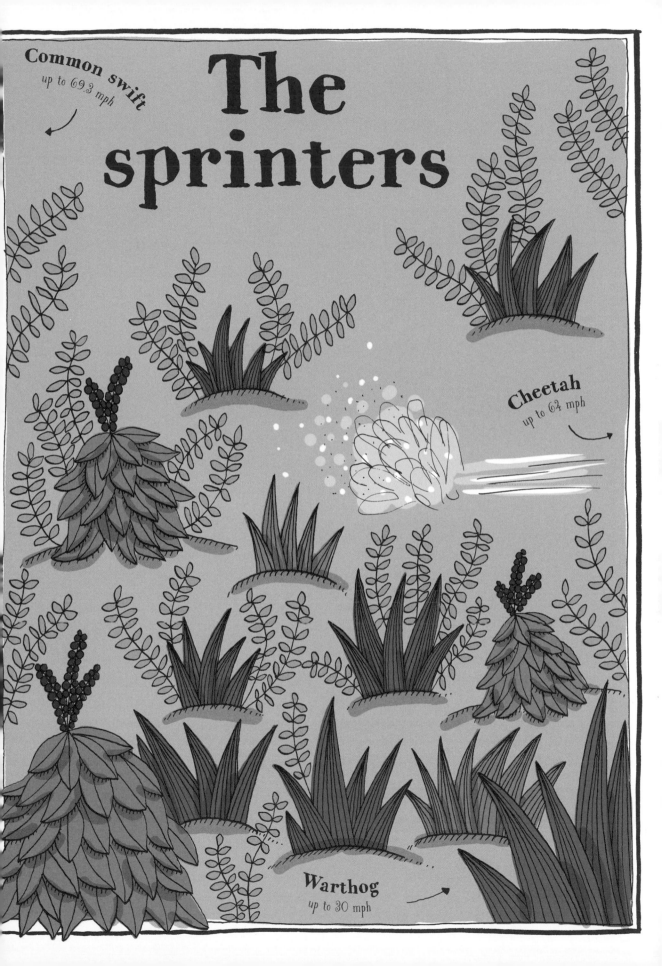

The sprinters

Common swift
up to 69.3 mph

Cheetah
up to 64 mph

Warthog
up to 30 mph

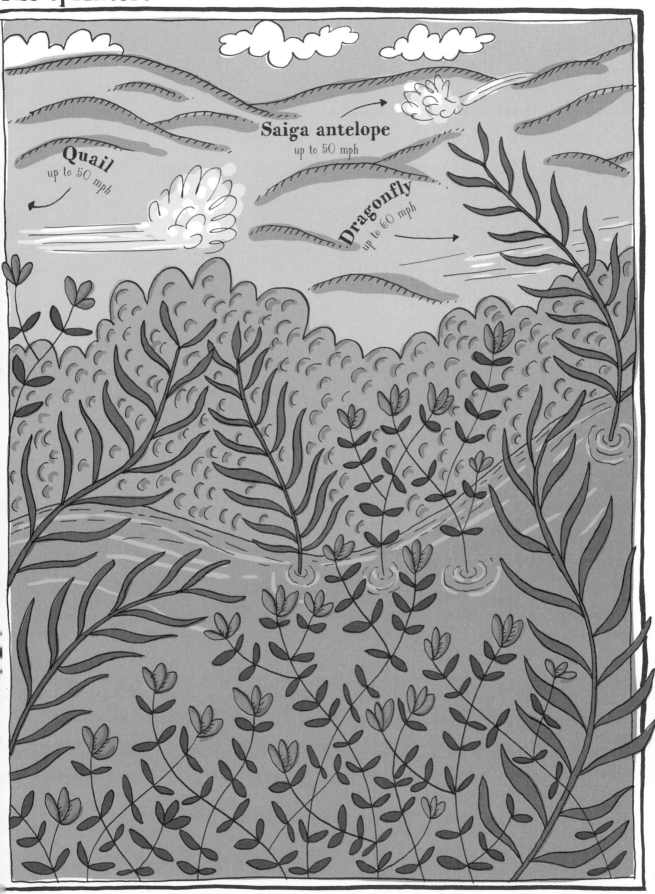

Saiga antelope
up to 50 mph

Quail
up to 50 mph

Dragonfly
up to 60 mph

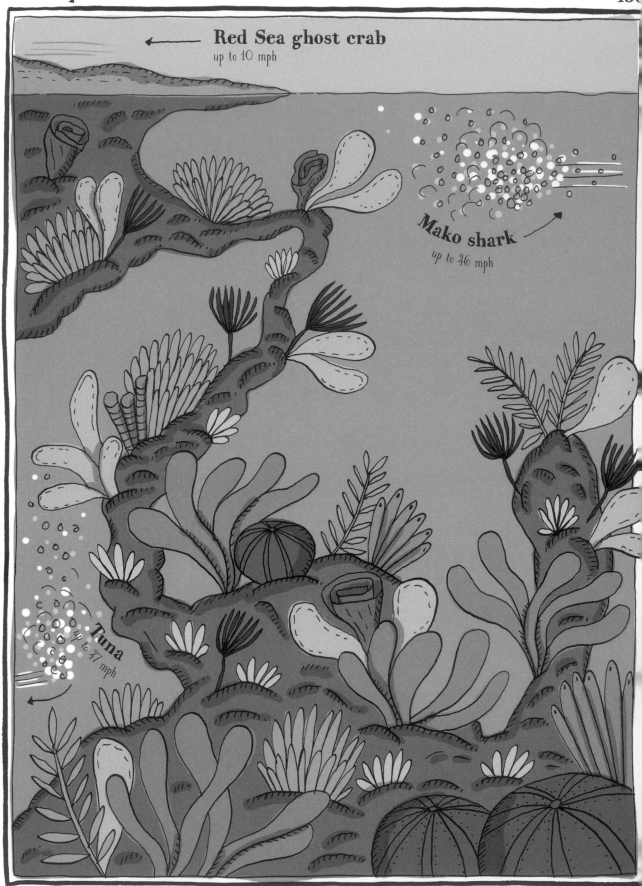

Red Sea ghost crab
up to 10 mph

Mako shark
up to 46 mph

Tuna
up to 47 mph

Common ostrich up to 43 mph

Rhinoceros up to 30 mph

Greater roadrunner up to 26 mph

The striped

Grevy's zebra

Aardwolf

Striped hyena

Moorish idol

Copperband butterfly fish

Sheepshead

Fiji banded iguana

Bandy-bandy

Banded sea krait

Leopard ground squirrel

Barred antshrike

Numbat

Banded mongoose

Scarce swallowtail butterfly

Checkered beetle

Striped cucumber beetle

Minstrel bug

Colorado potato beetle

The unlucky

Rock dove
believed to carry diseases

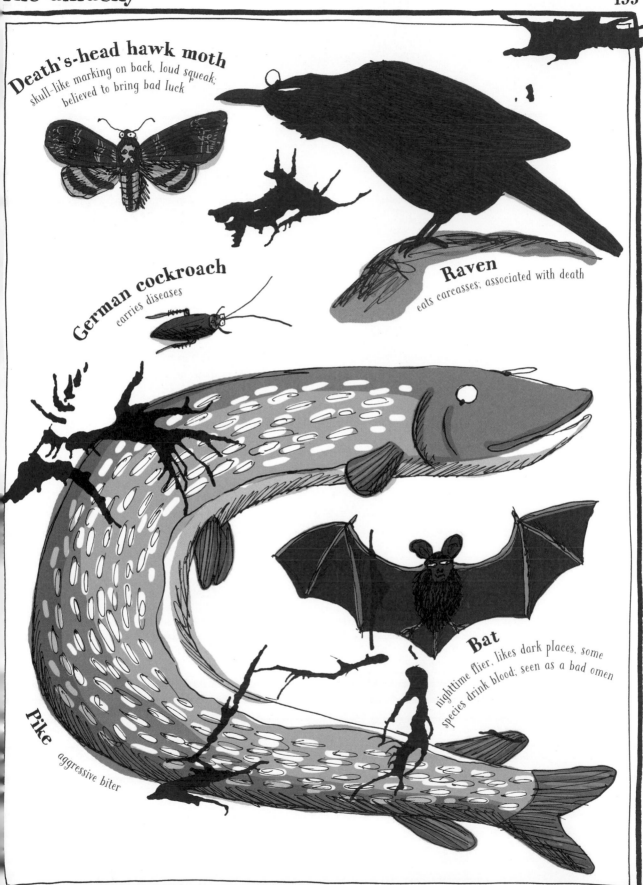

Death's-head hawk moth
skull-like marking on back, loud squeak; believed to bring bad luck

German cockroach
carries diseases

Raven
eats carcasses; associated with death

Bat
nighttime flier, likes dark places, some species drink blood; seen as a bad omen

Pike
aggressive biter

Great white shark attacks humans more than any other shark

Coypu carries diseases and damages crops

Wolf feared in many societies across the world

Tawny owl omen of bad luck

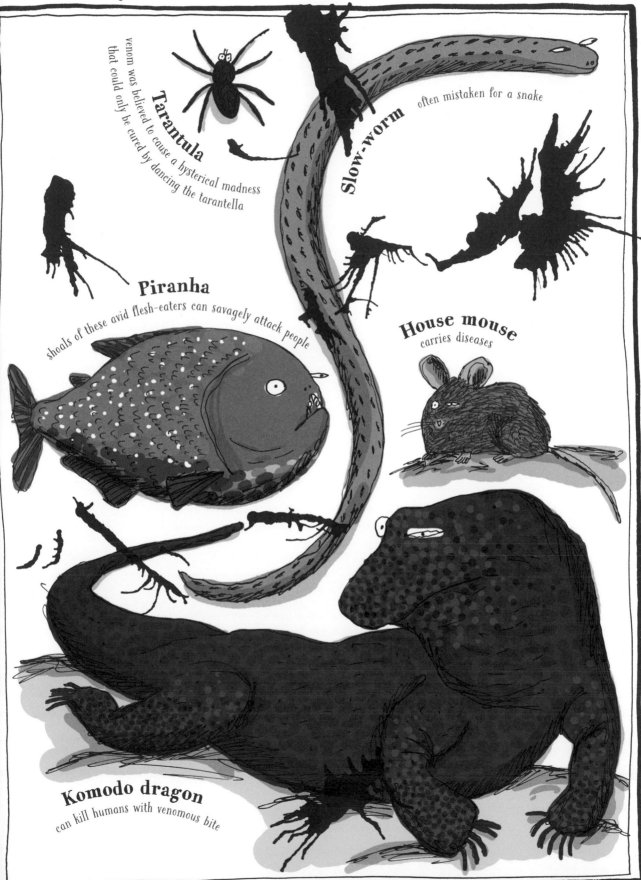

Tarantula
venom was believed to cause a hysterical madness that could only be cured by dancing the tarantella

Slow-worm often mistaken for a snake

Piranha
shoals of these avid flesh-eaters can savagely attack people

House mouse
carries diseases

Komodo dragon
can kill humans with venomous bite

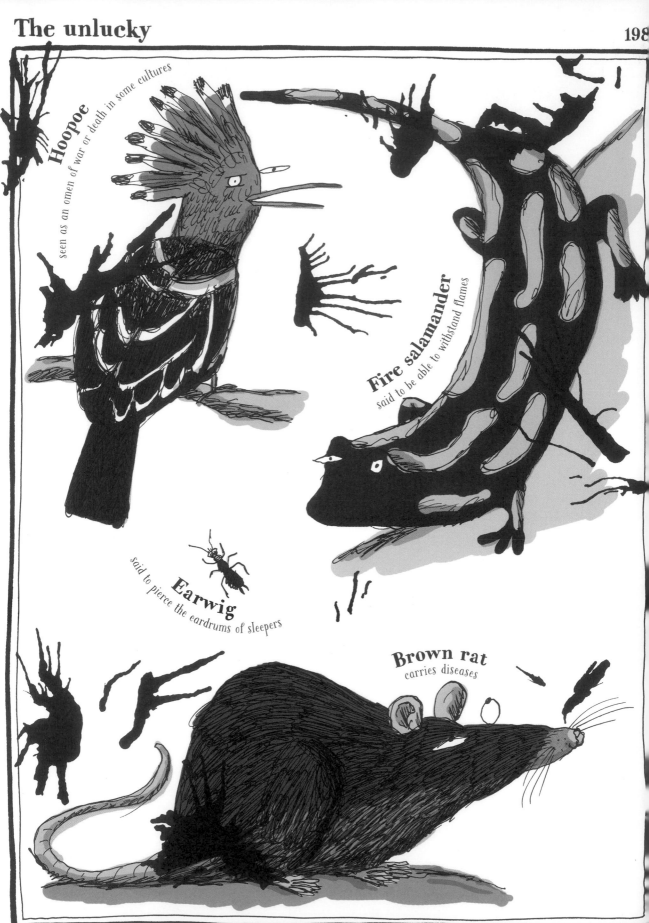

Hoopoe
seen as an omen of war or death in some cultures

Fire salamander
said to be able to withstand flames

Earwig
said to pierce the eardrums of sleepers

Brown rat
carries diseases

The vanished

Dodo
† between 1662 and 1681

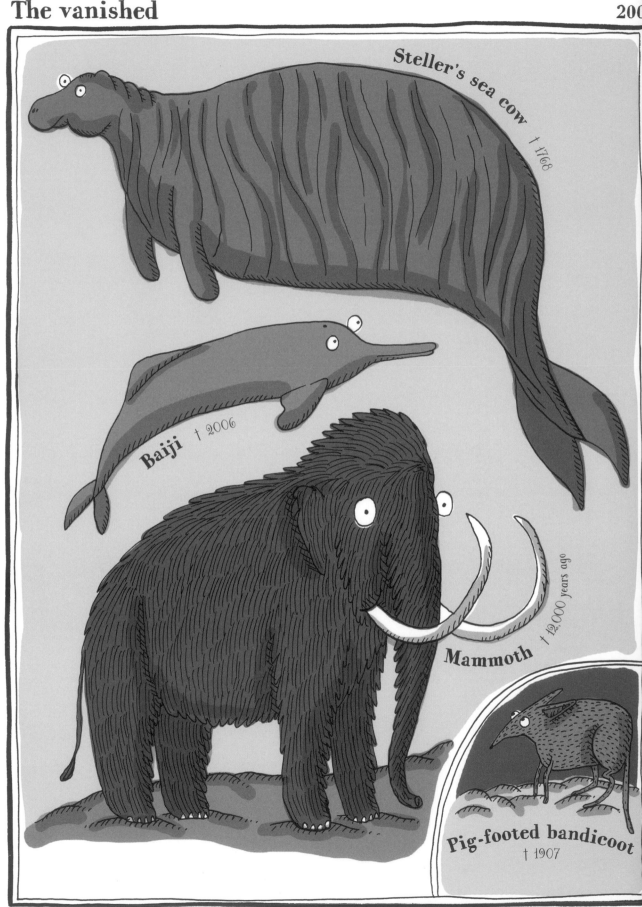

Steller's sea cow † 1768

Baiji † 2006

Mammoth † 12,000 years ago

Pig-footed bandicoot
† 1907

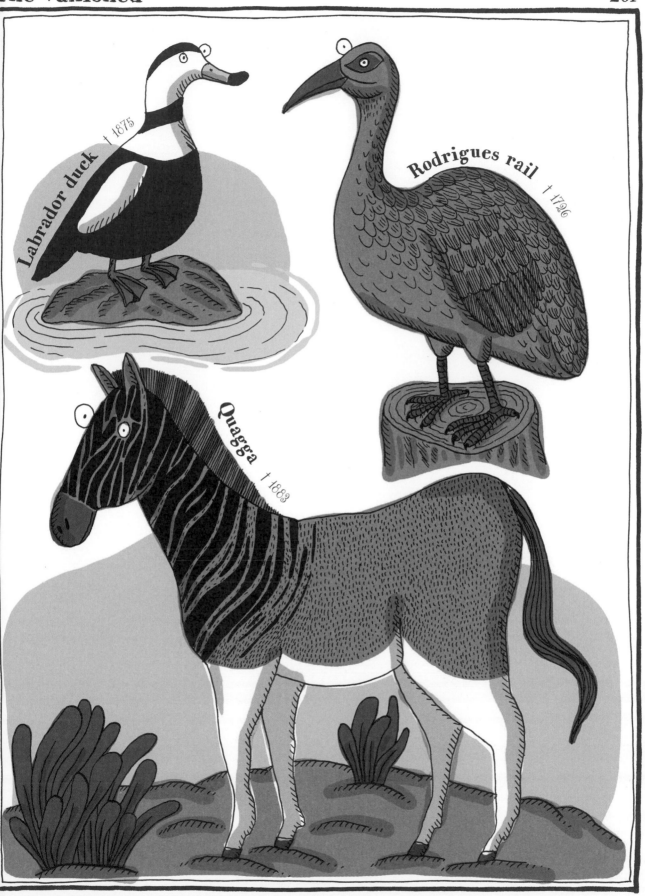

Labrador duck † 1875

Rodrigues rail † 1726

Quagga † 1883

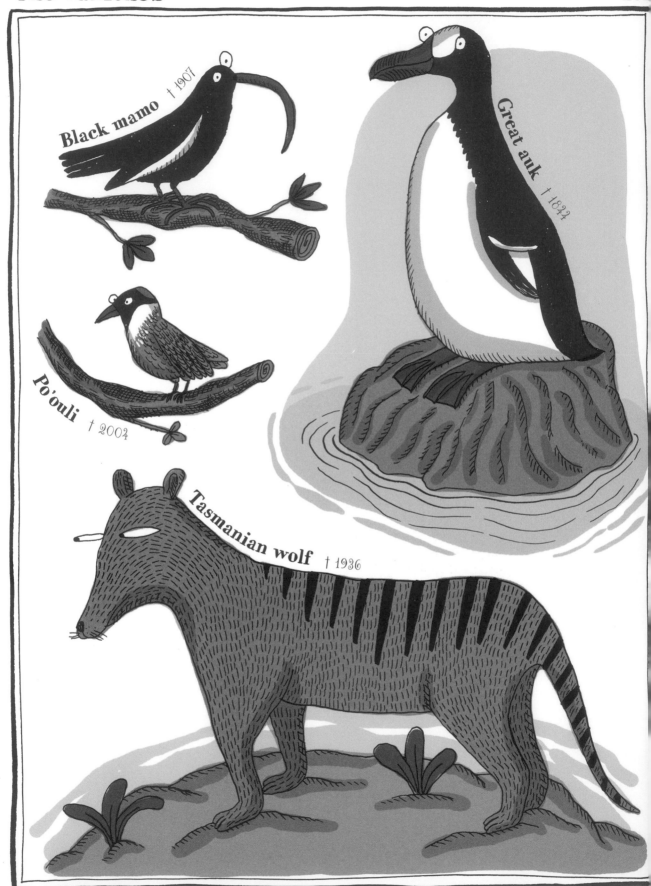

Black mamo † 1907

Great auk † 1844

Po'ouli † 2004

Tasmanian wolf † 1936

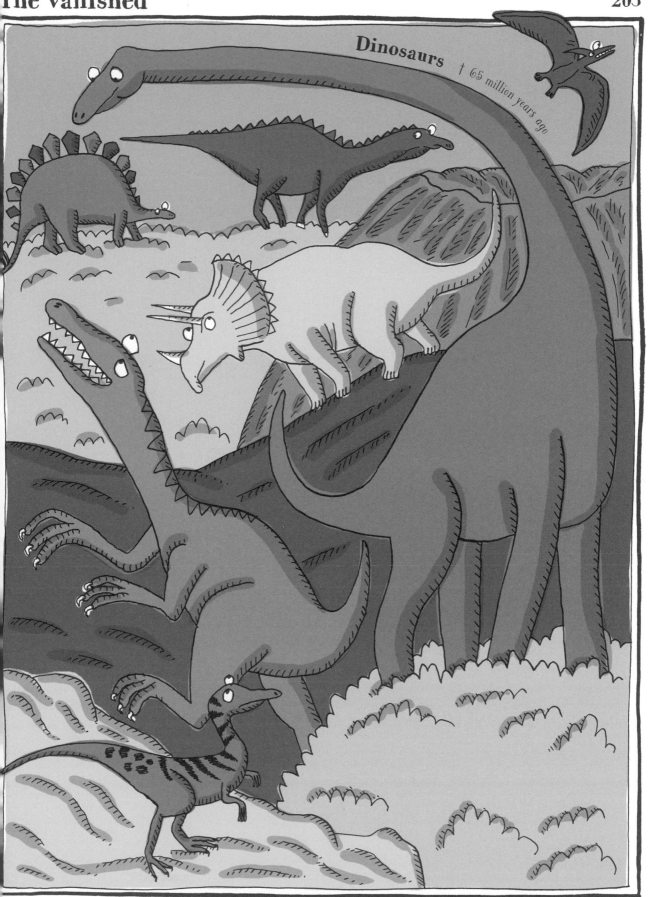

Dinosaurs † 65 million years ago

The voyagers

Common frog
travels to lay eggs

Blue wildebeest
migrates up to 1,000 miles each year
within east Africa

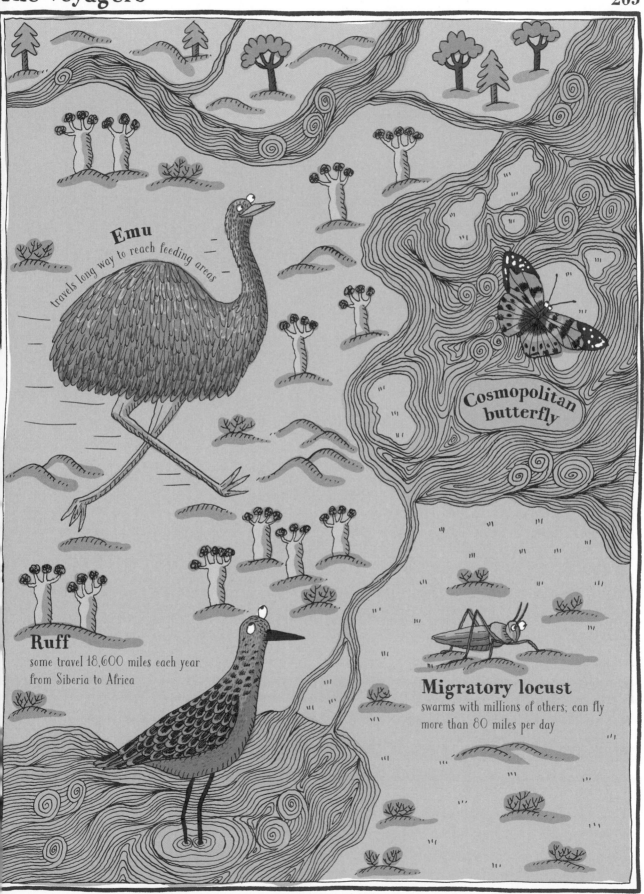

Emu
travels long way to reach feeding areas

Cosmopolitan butterfly

Ruff
some travel 18,600 miles each year
from Siberia to Africa

Migratory locust
swarms with millions of others; can fly
more than 80 miles per day

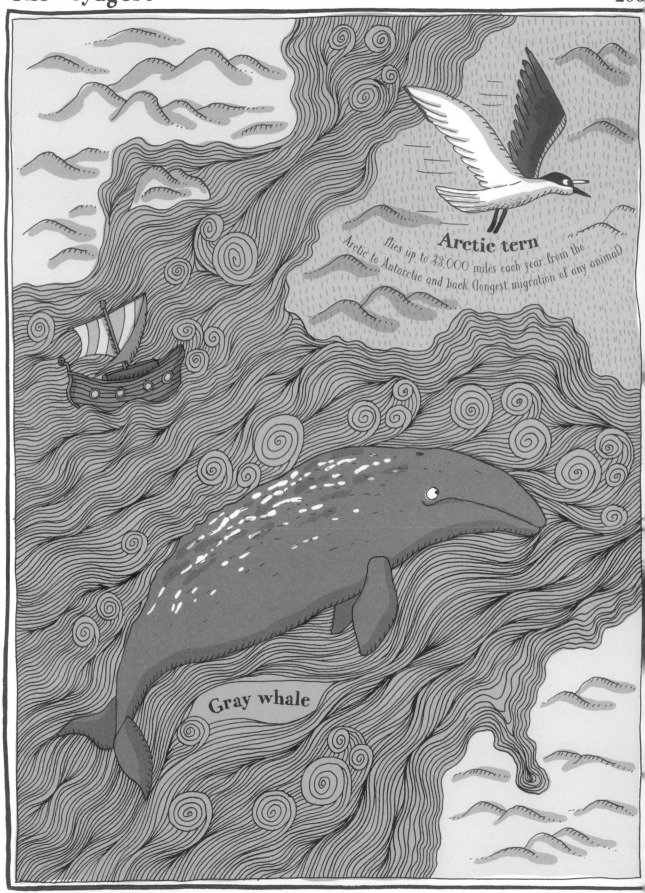

Arctic tern
flies up to 23,000 miles each year from the Arctic to Antarctic and back (longest migration of any animal)

Gray whale

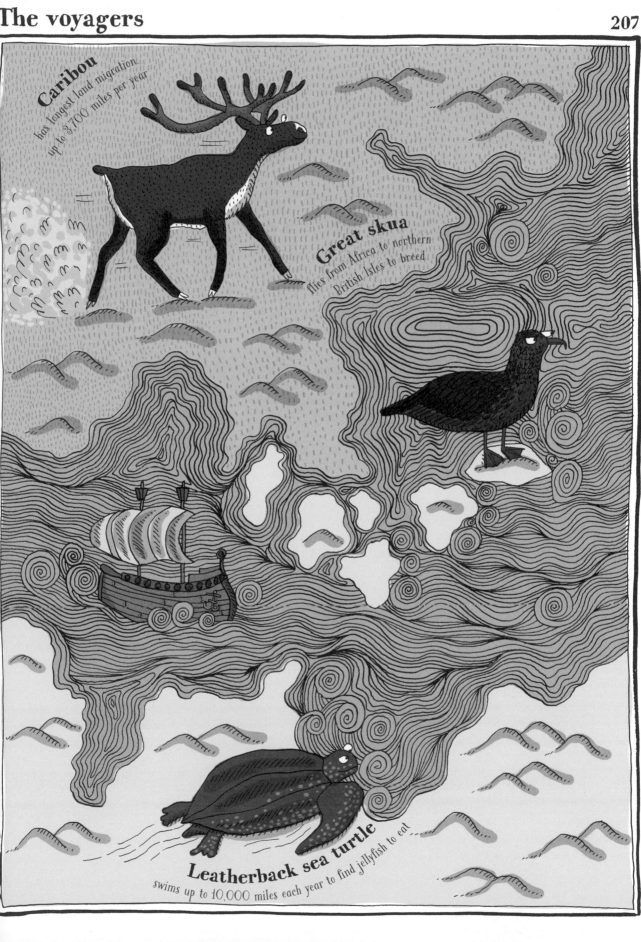

Caribou
has longest land migration,
up to 3,700 miles per year

Great skua
flies from Africa to northern
British Isles to breed

Leatherback sea turtle
swims up to 10,000 miles each year to find jellyfish to eat

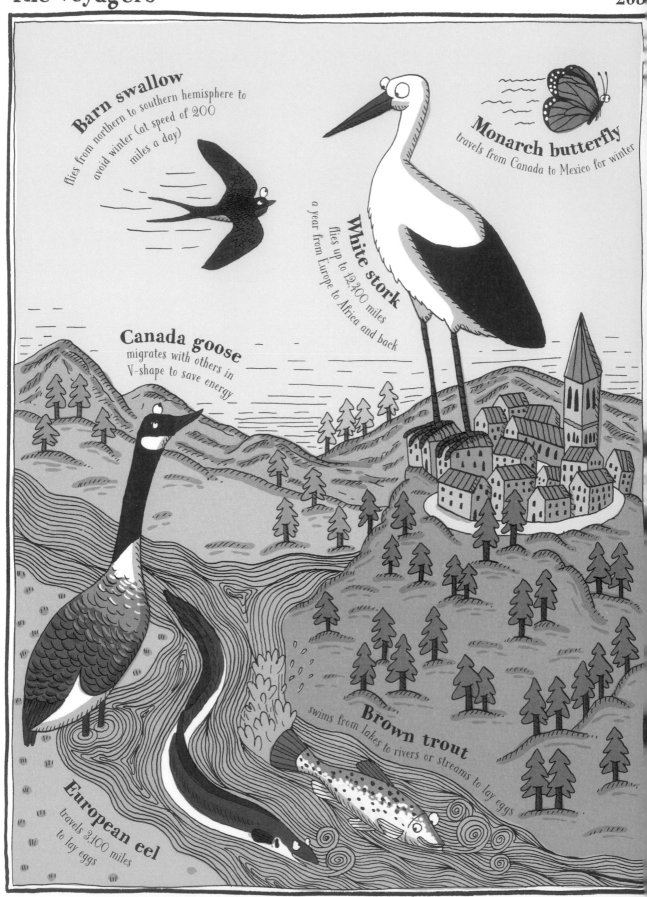

Barn swallow
flies from northern to southern hemisphere to avoid winter (at speed of 200 miles a day)

Monarch butterfly
travels from Canada to Mexico for winter

White stork
flies up to 12,400 miles a year from Europe to Africa and back

Canada goose
migrates with others in V-shape to save energy

Brown trout
swims from lakes to rivers or streams to lay eggs

European eel
travels 3,100 miles to lay eggs

Acknowledgments

My heartfelt thanks:
to the jury of the City and State of Geneva's 2011 grant for book illustration,
Jean Wüest, biologist, for his valuable corrections,
Cecile Koepfli (with the help of Emily and Lucia), Mirjana and Peggy Adam Farkas,
for their help with the coloring of some families

and also:
to my favorite sister,
my mother and my father for their constructive criticism and unconditional support,
Aldo for his advice and his comforting presence,
and to all my friends for their help and encouragement, many and varied:
Alain, Bichon, Anne HB, Aurélia, Barbara, Benjamin, Cécile, Cristina, Franky,
Ignacio, Jean-Marie, Jess, Matthew, Melanie, Mirjana, Moudja, Olga, Peggy, and Valerie

—A.B.

Index

Wide Eyed Editions
www.quarto.com

Creaturepedia © Editions La Joie de Lire SA 2013

Illustrated by Adrienne Barman
Designed by Pascale Rosier

First published in Switzerland in 2013 under the title *Drôle d'encyclopédie*
by Editions La Joie de Lire SA, 5 Chemin Neuf, CH-1207 Genève, Switzerland

First published in the United States by Wide Eyed Editions,
an imprint of The Quarto Group,
100 Cummings Center, Suite 265D, Beverly, MA 01915 USA.
www.quarto.com

All rights reserved. No part of this publication may be reproduced, stored in a retrieval system,
or transmitted, in any form or by any means, electronic, mechanical, photocopying,
recording, or otherwise, without prior written permission from the publisher.

LOC number pending

ISBN 978-0-7112-9578-0

Illustrated digitally

Set in Didodot and Bookeyed Martin

Manufactured in Guangdong, China TT042024

1 3 5 7 9 8 6 4 2